Too Big, Boring
Planning and Design Tools to Combat Monotony, the Too-big House, and Teardowns

LANE KENDIG

TABLE OF CONTENTS

CHAPTER 1

Defining the Problem

Little boxes on the hillside,
Little boxes made of ticky-tacky,
Little boxes, little boxes
Little boxes, all the same.

The song "Little Boxes," made famous by Pete Seeger in the 1960s, still rings true in many communities today despite the honest efforts of many home builders to provide variety in their product line. Figure 1-1 shows housing from the era of the song; Figure 1-2 illustrates current "not so little boxes."

Figure 1-1: Little Boxes.

Figure 1-2: Big Boxes.

Particularly at the lower end of the market, homes built today often resemble the little green houses that come in a Monopoly board game set, a problem hereinafter referred to as Monopoly-set housing. A symptom of this problem is that the general architectural quality of entry- and mid-level housing has declined over the years in terms of the overall attention given to architectural details, as can be seen by comparing the plans and elevations for a small 1920s bungalow with those of a modern starter house.

Since the end of World War II, when the national priority was to mass produce housing for returning veterans, the size of housing units has been increasing. The National Association of Home Builders (NAHB), as quoted in the June 10, 2001, *New York Times* business section, noted that the average size of a house has grown from 983 square feet in 1950 to more than 2,200 square feet in 2000. Since typically the size of the lots has not changed much, the scale of housing in relationship to the lot area creates a more crowded environment and often results in a more urban character. This problem is found at all price levels. Consequently, "McMansions" or "starter castles" (hereinafter the too-big house) may result in a community character very different from the one defined by the historical neighborhood pattern and zoning district regulations.

The too-big house creates a more complex series of problems in successful neighborhoods, both in cities and suburbs. First, neighborhood desirability brings increased housing values that when combined with the presence of older homes, which have smaller rooms and limited storage capacity, eventually leads to competition for housing and, consequently, conditions favorable for teardowns. Typically, older houses cover only a fraction of the buildable area created by setback regulations in the local zoning code. Thus, a neighborhood of one-story, 1,200-square-foot ranch homes could be confronted with two-story units of 3,000 or more square feet that are clearly out of character with the existing community. The problem of teardowns is complicated by the fact that the phenomenon is almost completely driven by real estate economics and lifestyle preferences. Teardowns or extensive remodeling need not be a problem if well done; in fact, economically they are a statement of community success. Having neighborhoods renew without degenerating to slums is highly desirable. It is where the character of a good neighborhood is destroyed that teardowns are a problem.

Two problems—monotony and the Monopoly-set house—are clearly related to the mass production of housing. Therefore, before discussing these two problem areas in detail, there is a discussion of the root cause.

The problem of the too-big house, on the other hand, crosses all sectors of the housing market and has very different antecedents than the monotony or Monopoly-set house. And the teardown problem is a variant of the too-big house. The cause of these issues will be covered as part of the problem discussions in each chapter.

Monotony in appearance and Monopoly-set housing were problems usually found in the entry- and mid-level housing markets. Today, with the advent of luxury production builders, these problems are also surfacing in the upper levels of the market. In other words, these issues continue to confront communities. Fortunately, anti-monotony codes (sometimes called monotony codes), bulk ordinances, landscaping, and variable lot requirements are all tools the planner can use to address them. In addition, for very large projects or high-end projects with substantial architectural budgets, the New Urbanist pattern book can be a useful tool. These and other regulatory approaches will be discussed in this report.

MASS PRODUCTION

The major source of the monotony and Monopoly-set house problems is the large-scale production of housing. The problem noted in the song "Little Boxes," while it reflected on mid-twentieth-century suburban housing developments, did not originate then. It could be seen in large-scale urban developments before World War I, and it continues today.

Indigenous communities (i.e., those that have grown slowly over 100 or more years), on the other hand, seem to have a charm not found in large-scale production developments. Whether they are in Europe, Africa, or the United States, indigenous communities grow slowly and, as a result, have strong attraction and interest levels, even when technology and building materials are limited to a very narrow palette. Typically, in indigenous communities, there is a unity of overall character, while strong variety and interest work to create an environment where nobody would think about "looking for your house by the color of the door," a phrase that evolved from a series of stories about how owners in communities marked by monotonous house design painted their garage doors or entryways different colors so that someone coming home late at night (perhaps slightly inebriated) could identify his or her house.

The Levittowns, in both New York and Pennsylvania, were massive production developments created by a large-scale developer seeking to meet a very specific market of World War II veterans returning to start families and careers. At the time, Federal Housing Administration (FHA) loans were made only for houses between 800 and 1,100 square feet (Friedman 2000). The housing was all entry-level, and the need was very great. Levittown

Monotony in appearance and Monopoly-set housing were problems usually found in the entry- and mid-level housing markets. Today, with the advent of luxury production builders, these problems are also surfacing in the upper levels of the market.

and its successors are frequently admonished or criticized principally because mass-produced housing tends to create problems of monotony or the Monopoly-set house. Remember the famous Henry Ford line, "You can have any color as long as it is black." The production builder or developer is involved in mass production; their rationale is to cut costs by standardizing production. It is far easier to introduce variety into cars by using colors than it is into houses where bright, flashy colors are generally not acceptable.

The mass production of housing developments must be compared to the indigenous small town or village in order to understand the difference in outcomes. The first difference is the speed of development. Levittown, for example, took three years to complete while an indigenous community would develop over a period of at least a century. Even when homes in an indigenous community were built from stock plans or from a Sears catalog model, they were custom ordered and built one at a time. If two families ordered homes from the Sears catalog, they were unlikely to be built on adjoining lots. Homes built decades apart for different families added greatly to diversity.

A second difference between large-scale production housing and indigenous housing is related to who built the house. Over a period of 100 years or more, it is likely that many different builders construct the houses in a community. Very few of these builders erected more than a handful of houses in a community. It may even be that owners and their friends built many of the houses rather than having them built by a contractor. This diversity in builders added to the variety of housing stock. Speculative home builders (i.e., developers who put in roads and sold lots, but who either did not build homes or had only a small construction operation) sold lots to prospective homeowners, who then contracted with a builder, or to home builders who constructed only a few homes per year. Some speculative home builders would not sell more than a couple of contiguous lots to a single builder. Again, time was a major factor with speculative home builders. While some speculative home builders sold out large subdivisions in a few years time, many did not. Even when they did sell out, many lots remained undeveloped for years. In some cases, lot owners would hold land for long periods of time while saving money to build their dream homes. Moreover, small builders typically took several years to build after purchasing lots. The end result in a project was a far greater diversity in the housing design.

A small builder who builds one to 10 homes a year does not have to worry about standardization. Such a builder can function much like a custom home builder because the capacity for production is restricted by a limited crew that, by and large, does the whole house, rather than a number of teams that each specialize in different aspects of the job.

Cost is another element that leads to monotony. A production builder seeks to control costs in two ways: by getting better prices through high-volume purchases of materials and by controlling product design. The large- and, even, medium-production builders expect to build hundreds of units a year; at this scale, there is a very different set of economics. The ability to dig and pour foundations and follow with carpenters, plumbers, electricians, dry wallers, and finishers is what enables them to produce units at the best price. For example, if the foundation crew must custom measure each form, it will work slower, resulting in higher costs and a more expensive unit. The same process holds true for most other parts of the development. Likewise, if trusses are all the same, mistakes are reduced and installation is expedited. Clearly, there are strong economic reasons for monotony in production housing.

Homes built decades apart for different families added greatly to diversity.

Today, there is another element contributing to escalating housing costs—the market desires the biggest possible box. In seeking to maximize square footage, architecture suffers. This explains part of the monotony and Monopoly-set problems. In response to the demand for more volume, home builders look for other ways to keep the structure affordable. Eliminating trim and repeating identical units are two ways home builders attempt to cut costs.

This is not intended to be an apology or an excuse for monotonous or Monopoly-set housing. However, it is important to understand some of the reasons why these conditions arise. It is also important to note that the consumer plays a significant role in this trend. If Americans demanded better design, the market would respond. Currently, the trade-off of maximum space or volume versus design is heavily in favor of volume, which, when combined with mass production, is an underlying root cause for the problems of monotony, Monopoly-set housing, and the too-big house.

MONOTONY

Monotony, defined as producing a lack of interest in detail or other design elements, is at one end of the design spectrum. At the other end is an equally undesirable condition—chaos. In the middle is harmony. Subdivisions are monotonous because the same limited numbers of house models are repeated over and over with inadequate differentiation. In many cases, particularly on smaller lots, the differentiation between models, while it may be obvious in floor plans, is less evident in the elevations of the buildings (Figures 1-3 and 1-4).

Today, there is another element contributing to escalating housing costs—the market desires the biggest possible box. In seeking to maximize square footage, architecture suffers.

Figure 1-3: The problem of monotony in mass-built 1960s subdivisions.

Figure 1-4: The problem of monotony in new housing.

As was discussed above, mass-produced housing requires repetition of a limited number of models, which are buildings with different floor plans. If the models are somewhat distinctive, the problem is less daunting. However, the differences between models are often insignificant, perhaps a variance of two to four feet in width, which amounts to 4 to 8 percent for a 50-foot-wide building. This difference is often difficult to detect. Likewise, the buildings generally use similar roof trusses, so height is not variable, and the models often have a very common bulk. With trivial variations in facades, the result, predictably, is monotony.

In most suburban and many modern urban areas, garages face the street. This greatly affects the character of residential streets because a two-car garage is 20 to 24 feet in width and can easily represent 40 to 50 percent of the facade. Figure 1-5 shows how very little can be done to differentiate homes when half of their facades are identical regardless of the floor plan. On narrow lots, a garage located in front of the dwelling makes the problem worse.

Figure 1-5: Narrow house with facade dominated by garage door.

Many home builders are aware of this problem and have some form of internal anti-monotony standards they try to employ. If the variations do not truly create different houses, however, the effort will still result in monotonous developments. Developers who change roof trim and design, and who introduce options for building materials in trying to vary facades have been successful in some developments, but variety only in the front facades leaves the sides and rears of houses looking the same. The lack of 360-degree architecture may mean that houses in a development, when seen from a nearby viewpoint such as an arterial or collector road, look identical because the viewer sees only their rear. Even when home builders give a lot of attention to the front facades, the building heights and bulks are often nearly identical, so their effort is less effective than one would expect.

Some of the things that would contribute to greater diversity are difficult for the production builder to achieve. Significant variation in width, height, and bulk, for example, can prevent monotony, even if materials and style are very similar. But the production builder focuses on a specific segment of the market and a narrow price range, which makes significant differences between units difficult to achieve. Lastly, in too many communities, there is a lack of landscaping, which exposes the monotony to full view.

MONOPOLY-SET HOUSES

Homes that have been stripped down to cut costs, while providing maximum floor area, begin to look very much like the little green houses from the Monopoly set (Figure 1-6). This worsens the monotony effect by cutting back on design elements of the house and concentrating on maximum volume.

Figure 1-6: Monopoly-set houses (literally).

The original stick-built house typically had eaves that provided a shadow line, which added to the character of the house (Figure 1-7). While significant eaves were not part of all architectural styles, they were very common elements of most housing. Only the Cape Cod house tended not to have eaves or significant roof-wall interface detailing. Except in climates where overhangs are needed to shed water, the trend in entry-level and mid-level housing today has been to eliminate the eaves in order to cut costs. In Figure 1-8, the gable end has no shadow line and the non-gable side has a thin shadow line from gutters. Although this reduces the cost of materials for roof trusses, ventilation, and trim, it is unfortunate because the lack of a shadow line and trim at the roof-wall juncture greatly adds to the Monopoly-set appearance.

Figure 1-7: *Large eaves.*

Figure 1-8: *Inadequate eaves.*

The reliance on mass-produced roof trusses in place of site built framing also encourages the use of similar roof pitches throughout an entire project so that there is no variation in roof pitch and, often, only minor variation in roof height since the house widths are quite similar. Thus, houses are often simple, two-story rectangles with no differences in facades to provide interest (Figure 1-9). Even in much more expensive homes where the building coverages and shapes are similar, common roof pitches result in very similar masses, even where the developer is seeking variety (Figure 1-10).

Older homes with wood siding or masonry exteriors typically had trim around windows, which was essential to the construction and weatherproofing of the window. Additionally, in many house styles, shutters were a common design element. These details were carried around all four sides of the house because they served a function. The modern production house makes use of vinyl or aluminum siding and metal or metal-clad windows that can be

(Below) **Figure 1-9:** *The simple rectangles of the modern house;*
(right) **Figure 1-10:** *Identical or nearly equal mass.*

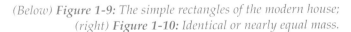

installed without framing or significant trim (Figure 1-11). As a result, windows often look like they were inserted by a punch, like holes cut in a pumpkin. In addition, unlike dwellings built in the past, there appears to be no rationale for the location of windows in relationship to each other.

Figure 1-11: Punch-out windows, lacking relationships.

Builders often install a dressed-up or false front. With this type of structure, the windows and front doors are trimmed and, in many instances, masonry is applied to the front. This dresses up the house from the street, but the false nature of the front (Figure 1-12) is painfully obvious as soon as the sides and rear of the house become visible (Figure 1-13). The false front cheapens the look of the rest of the house.

Figure 1-12: A "false" front.

Figure 1-13: The side and rear of the house featured in Figure 1-12.

These elements combine to make many houses an unattractive addition to the community. As with monotony, the lack of landscaping exposes all the faults of the house design to open view.

THE TOO-BIG HOUSE

Monster houses, McMansions, starter castles, or simply the too-big house are problems with recent housing construction. Since the production homes of the late 1940s and early 1950s, the average size of the American house has been increasing (U.S. Census 2000, C–25). The starter homes of these earlier years were small buildings, with small bedrooms and small closets, so that they sat quite nicely on the small suburban or urban lot (Figure 1-14). The size increase is dramatic (Table 1-1). A quick review of today's housing magazines and books reveals master bedrooms and bathrooms much larger than they were in the typical 1950s house. In other cases, the homes seem to be a statement of the owner's economic status, asking the viewer to look how tall, wide, and big my house is. The very real need for more storage space, combined with examples from the housing press and status-seeking owners, ensures that there will be continued pressure for ever-larger homes.

Figure 1-14: Starter houses in the 1950s were small and sat comfortably on small lots.

Figure 1-15: The McMansion, dominating the lot.

TABLE 1: HOUSE SIZE, 1950 to 2000			
	1950	2000	% change
Average house size	983 sq. ft.	2,265 sq. ft.	130
Changes in Rooms (percentage)			
2 or fewer bedrooms	66	11	-83
3 bedrooms	33	53	61
4 or more bedrooms	1	35	3,400
1.5 bathrooms or less	96	7	-93
2 bathrooms	3	38	1,167
2.5 bathrooms or more	1	56	5,500

Source: U.S. Census Bureau, C-25

The increase in floor area is aggravated by a trend to higher floor-to-floor heights. For many years, eight-foot ceilings, based on eight-foot studs, were the national standard. Today, even apartments are being built with nine- or 10-foot studs, raising the total height of the building and clearly increasing bulk. The two-story entry hall and other two-story spaces also increase the bulk of the home. Roof pitches, which do not need to exceed 5/12 (meaning five feet of rise over 12 feet of horizontal run, which is approximately 23 degrees or a 42 percent slope) except in the heaviest snow load areas, approach and, in some instances, exceed 12/12. The combination of increased floor area, increased ceiling heights, greater roof pitches, as well as multistory spaces greatly increases building bulk. This bungalow floor plan from the early part of the twentieth century clearly indicates that the ability to modify elevations with roof design is well understood (Figure 1-16).

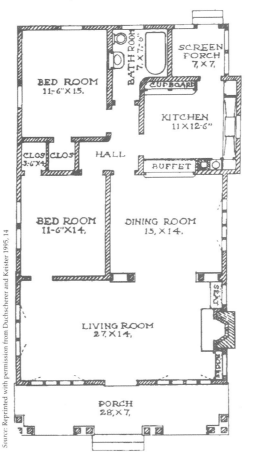

Figure 1-16: A bungalow floor plan from 1923 and the house that results indicates an understanding of roof design.

Source: Reprinted with permission from Duchscherer and Keister 1995, 14

Unfortunately, these trends have now reached the stage where the homes no longer fit the scale of the lots. A lot that had a very suburban character with homes built in the 1950s through the 1970s can take on an urban character with the larger, closely spaced homes built today. The shear mass of the building is the cause of this phenomenon. In brand new subdivisions, homes are built to fill the building pad within the setbacks. This has caused trouble in many communities where zoning prohibits decks in the setbacks.

This was not a problem in the past when the home filled only a portion of the building pad.

There have been previous markets or eras when large homes were built. However, in many of these older developments, there was a totally different approach to landscaping. Lots were landscaped for privacy, often by leaving the lot in trees (Figure 1-17) or with hedges or hedgerow plantings (Figure 1-18) along lot lines. Today, landscaping is limited to foundation plantings (Figure 1-19) and many homeowners leave the front relatively clear of vegetation, which frames and emphasizes the sheer bulk of the too-big house.

(Below, left) **Figure 1-17:** *Front landscaping used for privacy; (right, above)* **Figure 1-18:** *Hedgerows used to preserve privacy; (right, below)* **Figure 1-19:** *Foundation plantings framing and emphasizing the bulk of the too-big house.*

TEARDOWNS

The teardown is defined here as a too-big house built in the middle of an existing neighborhood where its scale destroys the neighborhood's character. All of the factors that have led to the too-big house are also operating in the case of teardowns. Unlike the too-big house in a greenfield or new subdivision, the teardown is, by definition, built in a neighborhood with a well-defined character.

Teardowns, for the most part, involve the demolition of an older housing unit on the property (thus the name teardown). Even though the house may be large, it must be treated as a separate issue from the too-big house because of the underlying economic factors. Many of these neighborhoods contain units built by production builders, typically between the 1930s to early 1970s. In these neighborhoods, the post-World War II entry-level housing (Figure 1-20) is particularly vulnerable. Likewise, in cities, small bungalows, along with 1950s houses, are vulnerable. Even in areas with three-story homes, however, the high ceilings and multistory spaces of the new McMansions can create a problem by destroying the strong roofline, without monotony, common to a block or neighborhood. The three-story urban houses of the late nineteenth or early twentieth century also had a common floor height and generally fairly rich and varied detailing. The combination of increased floor heights and cathedral ceilings in new housing results in a building whose height is that of a four-story building. This is quite different from the impact of towers or varied roof pitches found in older urban neighborhoods.

Even in areas with three-story homes, the high ceilings and multistory spaces of the new McMansions can create a problem by destroying the strong roofline, without monotony, common to a block or neighborhood.

Figure 1-20: An example of post-World War II housing—a prime candidate for a teardown.

It is vital to understand the teardown is an economic and lifestyle phenomena, not simply poor taste.

The increased need for storage, larger room sizes, taller ceilings, multi-story spaces, and steeper roof pitches are only part of the problem. Coupled with these symptoms are the needs and desires motivating landowners to build bigger houses. The real issue is pure economics. Teardowns often occur in old, desirable neighborhoods, such as suburban neighborhoods near train stations, neighborhoods in trendy communities, areas with waterfront lots, or neighborhoods with scenic views. Whether the value is created by the desirability of the neighborhood or by a physical element, such as an accessible waterfront, a driving force is the rising property values of the neighborhood. That said, teardowns are rarely a problem in less desirable neighborhoods and may, in fact, create the beginnings of an urban pioneering effort where building a new home is more affordable than it would be in a desirable neighborhood.

Before teardowns occur, there must be an appreciation in land values that dramatically alters the economics of the neighborhood. The location of the neighborhood and its perceived desirability drive the teardown phenomenon. Teardowns are more costly than similar too-big houses in greenfield settings. In addition to the cost of the land, the person purchasing a lot with the intention to tear down the existing unit must pay for the existing house. While the rule of thumb is that the value of the land is generally 25 percent of the total value, for the teardown, the land value may be more than 50 percent of the total value. The person buying the teardown at this inflated value (relative to the house) wants a house in keeping with the land value. Thus, unless they insist on a design that respects the neighborhood character and architecture, the result is a too-big house.

There is no question teardowns are often out of keeping with the character of the surrounding neighborhood. They will be measurably out of character when one uses any of the following indicators to compare the teardown with its neighbors: building floor areas, floor area ratios, volumes, building volume ratios, or site volume ratios.

At this point, it is vital to understand the teardown is an economic and lifestyle phenomena, not simply poor taste. One would expect home builders to oppose teardown regulations because such regulations affect a profitable market. The great difficulty is that the neighborhood is unlikely to be uniform in its attitude toward teardowns. While there will be neighbors who are outraged by the teardowns and complain the units are out of keeping with the character of the existing neighborhood, there may be others who support the change and want to profit from the neighborhood's growing attractiveness and increased property values.

The opponents of teardowns have important economic concerns as well as design concerns. First, land values will go up dramatically and, in turn, property taxes will also rise. The increase in taxes may threaten older residents with fixed or lower incomes, forcing them to sell or affecting their standard of living. Consequently, those who feel threatened economically may join forces with those who simply want to preserve the character of the neighborhood.

Tearing down the obsolescent house is an economic decision and a practical solution. Similarly, another group within the community, perhaps those of moderate means who bought before land prices began their drastic increase, may see an opportunity to profit. They may not have the money to tear down the existing unit or to make dramatic alterations, but they may see the run-up in value as an opportunity to make a quick profit, which they can then use to move up to a larger, more modern, or just different house elsewhere. This group will side with those who do not want limitations on teardowns and might even seek zoning changes to allow increased bulk.

The economics of the neighborhood and the way people choose sides make the teardown issue very different from the concerns about the too-big house. It also makes it a highly political issue, rather than a technical zoning issue. It shares common elements with gentrification problems in neighborhoods, even when there are no socioeconomic or racial overtones.

The opponents of teardowns have important economic concerns as well as design concerns.

CHAPTER 2

Monotony

onotony is found in subdivisions or neighborhoods where many homes in close proximity are
identical or very similar. Similarity in style, however, does
not automatically lead to monotony. Strategic use of different models and careful detailing can make a neighborhood
composed of houses built in the same style interesting and
harmonious.

Monotony is an aesthetic term that describes one end of a continuum. At the other end of the continuum is chaos. It is a slightly unusual continuum in that both ends are undesirable while the middle condition, harmony, is desired. Many elements of house design provide opportunities to create a harmonious diversity of housing in a neighborhood. A failure to use these tools leads to a sameness reducing the distinction and identity of individual units to the point where the community has no definable character. The impact of monotony is most noticeable when developments are new. Over time, residents customize their home or lot. The examples in Figure 2-1 illustrate a series of minor changes or cosmetic changes, such as color or painting scheme, that relieve some of the monotony. In addition, when canopy trees shelter buildings and individual yard landscaping has matured, the monotony problem is softened. Although they help, time and individual customization should not be viewed as a totally acceptable cure.

Figure 2-1: Cosmetic changes can break up monotony but are not a completely acceptable cure for the problem.

Density can also has a significant impact on monotony. Narrow lots, for example, reduce the width of the unit and give the architect less to work with to create interest. Higher density means that more dwellings are visible at one time and, thus, monotony is more obvious to the viewer.

TWO DESIGN APPROACHES FOR ADDRESSING MONOTONY

Administration of anti-monotony codes ultimately requires a system whereby the local government can review proposed unit types to ensure that developers and buyers are planning to build a unit meeting the code. Few builders will have enough model types to adequately meet the goals of the anti-monotony regulations, and as a result, they will have to create new facade designs sufficiently different to create visible distinctions between units.

There are two very different design approaches to preventing monotony: style and detailing. Each relies on a set of preapproved plans and elevations.

With the style approach, the builder offers the home buyer floor plans in different architectural styles modeled after historical periods, such as early colonial, romantic (for example, Greek Revival, stick Victorian, or Queen Anne Victorian), Tudor, mission, prairie, craftsman, or modern. Figure 2-2 illustrates the distinguishing elements of the different architectural styles. The community may approve elevations for a model representing adaptations of historical styles with differences significant enough that the units do not look the same. A good reference book may be needed; *A Field Guide to American Houses* by Virginia and Lee McAlester, for example, may be a useful resource.

The review of the proposed elevations needs to be rigorous, ensuring that the buildings really look different. There is a tendency to tack on a few inexpensive details from a style that do not really alter the home. Figures 2-3, 2-4, and 2-5 show what supposedly are three different facades, each in a different style. What resulted in this application was "neo-nothingness" that is devoid of style and provides a very weak change in character. Note the same roof pitch and same double-hung widows are used on all the buildings. The result is none of the buildings really look like the style they purport to be.

One thing making the style approach desirable is that many historical styles used various design details as differentiating factors. One example is distinction in roof pitch, which affects building bulk. The Tudor house has steep roof pitches, often 12/12, while the craftsman has flat roof pitches near 5/12 where snow requires that homes employ such a roof pitch and even flatter where snow is not an issue. Another example is the use of many different window types. Prairie houses typically have casement windows, where Victorian and romantic styles use double-hung windows. Given the richness of style differences, it is important that more than cameo detailing is used to achieve the desired impact. On the other hand, the disadvantage of this approach is that it may not promote community harmony in architecture. Units may have strikingly different appearances, so that while monotony is avoided, a hint of chaos may be evident.

Source: Reprinted with permission from Duchscherer and Keister 1995, 32

Figure 2-2: The distinguishing elements of the different architectural style.

(Left) Figure 2-3: A "prairie" house; *(center) Figure 2-4:* A "Tudor" house; *(right) Figure 2-5:* A "Victorian" house.

The detailing approach uses detailing within a particular style to create unity and interest. The developer typically will pick a style and then manipulate design elements to make units with the same floor plan look quite different. This approach is more difficult to use than the style approach because a host of minor elements must be manipulated to create visible differences. At the same time, the units need to remain true to a theme. Avoiding monotony is a problem because changing some elements will mean essentially changing the style; for example, significant variation in roof pitch cannot be made without destroying a basic element of a style. As a result, a regulatory system used to evaluate differentiation must include a range of variables that can be manipulated to avoid monotony but still preserve style. Furthermore, any notable difference between models may end up being difficult to detect if a particular style has strong unifying features.

Some things can be done to modify the two approaches. It may be possible to pick styles common to a time period and found mixed together in older communities. For example, mixing various nineteenth century romantic styles (such as Early Revival, Greek Revival, and Italianate Revival) will work because, while each style is different, there are strong affinities in materials and appearance so as to look harmonious.

Another style-based approach has been used successfully where the site plan uses housing clusters on cul-de-sacs or loop roads. Here, style differentiates the clusters so that each cluster makes a different statement. Within the cluster, detailing, floor plan changes, the relatively small number of units, and differences in orientation help avoid monotony. Figures 2-6 to 2-8 show three cul-de-sacs from the Wood Creek Court in Lincolnshire, Illinois. This development has eight cul-de-sacs each with eight to 12 dwelling units and only four models. Within the clusters, there are units whose orientation—front, side, or internal corner—make it very difficult to see that each unit has the same floor plan. The fact that there are fewer than a dozen units with a similar architectural style reduces the scale and potential for monotony. In the next cluster, the same floor plan and the whole cluster have a different architectural style. Lastly, the detailing, landscaping, and garage orientation modify the units. In contrast, a 100-unit subdivision with the same historical style motif and four models will be far more difficult to control.

Figures 2-6, 2-7, and 2-8: The same architectural style can be used in a small number of units placed in a cluster, emloying orientation to make distinctions between houses that have the same floor plan. These clusters can then be dispersed in a subdivision, breaking up monotony in the subdivision as a whole.

THE PRIMARY TOOLS FOR ADDRESSING MONOTONY

The primary tools for addressing monotony are varying floor plans, mass, height, and a more recent development phenomenon, the bonus room—a room added above the garage, which alters attic space and the mass and roof of the house. In addition, there are several different elements used to differentiate facades and distinguish between models. There is no real difference in application; namely, these tools can be used with either the style or detail approach discussed above.

Floor Plans

Floor plans are a critical element in the appearance of the facade. While it is not uncommon for a builder to have three to five floor plans in a development, it is important to determine if the plans actually create a significant visual difference. For example, in small homes with front-loading garages, the floor plan has little impact because the garage takes up more than half of the available facade and screens other changes in the floor plan. To have effect, the floor plans must be significantly different in ways visible on the front facade, such as changes in facade planes, location of entry, width of the unit, and front room placement. It is obvious a change in floor plan on the rear will not affect the front elevation. Where building widths are very similar, significant floor plan changes will be needed to differentiate facades. Slight changes to the dimensions of living rooms or dining rooms may have no impact at all on the façade. All too often, differences produced by such changes are relatively trivial and not noticeable to the casual observer.

Significant differences in the plane of the front elevation, as a result of changes in room arrangements, are quite effective. An L- or T-shape floor plan is easily distinguished from a rectangular building footprint. A note of caution: if the differences are small, such as only one foot or so, the changes will not be effective. Many ordinances require changes in plane in attached housing with little real effect other than making a jagged, monotonous building, rather than a flat, monotonous one. In attached housing, there must be variation between buildings as well as variation from unit to unit.

As was mentioned above, a change in the position or location of the entry into the house is quite effective in relieving monotony. It has a double impact because it will often change the general landscaping of the front yard as well as the building's elevation. If it also modifies the footprint shape, it will be even more effective. In this case, the size of the change is not as important as was the case with L- or T-shape buildings.

Mass

In older, speculative subdivisions where the lots were sold to different individuals or builders and built out over a period of time, the changing style and size of homes over several decades was often reflected in the mass of the buildings as well as in the architectural style. Nowadays, where the homes use common production floor plans, changing mass is very important to avoid monotony.

Figures 2-9, 2-10, and 2-11 show three views of a luxury production subdivision where building massing has overwhelmed the floor plan elevation as defined by the anti-monotony code. This subdivision was the village's first real production development with large homes on small lots. Prior to this development, most subdivisions had been custom or semi-custom projects, and the lots were twice as large. Houses averaged 1,000 to 1,500 square feet smaller in size.

This subdivision presents a confluence of monotony and the too-big house. In this production subdivision, a single builder constructed homes within a couple of years that show little difference in mass because their roof pitches and general floor arrangements are similar. In this case, the builder did not employ two very important methods of altering mass—height (floors) and lot width (building width). Instead, there has been a reliance on difference in floor area, which does not necessarily make for a visual difference and a difference is in depth of the unit, which may have little impact on the front elevation. In both cases, the result is that the mass of individual houses appears quite similar.

Figures 2-9, 2-10, and 2-11: building massing in this subdivision overwhelms the floor plan, resulting in a confluence of monotony and the too-big house.

Height

In the modern subdivision, it is common to see relatively similar building masses in terms of floor area and building height. The ranch house, Cape Cod, or tri-level of the 1950s and 1960s had very different looks because they had different heights. The dominance of a straight two-story unit results in very similar roof peaks. The increased floor-to-floor height of recent years makes a great deal of difference in infill situations but has little impact in production subdivisions where most homes have similar floor-to-ceiling heights. The increased popularity of steep roof pitches has added to the problem. On rear elevations, the massing is often made worse by a whole row of buildings with walk-out basements, creating the mass of a three-story building.

A standard that requires a mix of ranch, 1.5-story, and two-story floor plans can be quite successful. Clearly, a ranch is very different from a two-story home (Figure 2-12). This is most effective for housing with similar floor areas. In luxury housing, on the other hand, a mere change in stories may not be as effective. When buildings were relatively shallow (24 to 30 feet), a Cape Cod with a half-story second floor was visibly quite different than the ranch. Today, the combination of larger homes, steeper roof pitches, and cathedral ceilings complicates the issue. It may be difficult to differentiate a 1.5-story unit from a two-story unit due to similar roof heights created by large front-to-rear distances.

Roof pitch is an effective tool for dealing with monotony when buildings have the same general footprint. The relatively shallow roof pitches (5/12 or less) result in low buildings, while the homes built in an English

Figure 2-12: Variation in unit height is very effective in preventing monotony.

Tudor style with roof pitches of 12/12 or greater produce very tall buildings. On a house with a depth of 36 feet, a 5/12 roof pitch produces a roof peak roughly 7.5 feet high. At 9/12, the peak is 13.5 feet; at 12/12, it is 18 feet. This approach can be used to calculate the difference in resulting roof heights. A change in pitch by 1 in 12 is a rise of 0.08333 feet per every two feet in building width measured at the gable end. Thus in a building 32 feet wide, changing the roof pitch from 5/12 to 6/12 results in a change of 1.33 feet (32/2 x .0833 = 1.33)

Bonus Rooms

Bonus rooms are rooms built over the garage, or less frequently, at the front of the house. These additions contribute to bulk. Technically, bonus rooms are a floor plan option, but care is needed to determine how they are best used. They are difficult to treat as a totally separate option because even though they have a very different roof line, the rest of the building is identical. If fewer than 25 percent of the models can have the bonus room, it can qualify as a different elevation. If more than 25 percent of the units are likely to have the bonus room, those units should be treated as a different model type, and the elevations need to have differentiating characteristics from the elevations without bonus rooms. It is best to allow bonus rooms on a limited number of models, so that elevations remain distinctive.

ELEMENTS OF DESIGN THAT CAN BE MANIPULATED TO PREVENT MONOTONY
Roof Orientation
Roof orientation refers to the relationship of the gable, either front or side, to the street. When the roof peak parallels the road (side gabled), the roof, in effect, adds the visual effect of another story. When it is perpendicular to the street (front gabled), the average height of the roof is automatically reduced by one half. This creates a very different feel and massing simply because the viewer's perception of the mass is altered. Figure 2-13 illustrates the difference between a building with the same ground floor plan and two different roof orientations.

Figure 2-13:
Orientation of the roof to the street can help prevent monotony.

Roof Styles
Roofs can be standard gabled in two orientations or they may be hipped, salt box, gambrel, mansard, flat, or a mix of any of these varieties. It is clear that a different roof type will create a different profile. This is most important where architectural style is used to create differences because roof form is consistent within a style. Similarly, a change in style may bring a large change in form. Gable orientation is the most important variable for the detail approach. In both approaches, the use of cross-shaped roofs, cross gables, or cross-hipped roofs can provide a different look. The use of dormers of various types can also create variety.

Building Orientation
The flipping of a model to a right-hand or left-hand orientation is a technique that adds variety. However, in large developments, this is a weak element because after you have seen the model in both orientations numerous times, it loses its effectiveness. The more complex the building, the more potential this technique offers since the building has greater potential to appear quite different from opposite perspectives.

On larger lots, a variation of flipping, rotation, is possible. By twisting the unit so it is not always parallel to the street, passersby are presented with a very different perspective. The most effective variation of this is a full 90-degree rotation. Full rotation means the architect must have a front door location that works on two walls or works with a front, side, or corner entry. All in all, building rotation is more effective than flipping, a fact that should be reflected in the scoring.

Trim Detailing
Trim detailing is probably the least expensive approach to creating variety, but one that is often a failure. Detailing applied without logic or consistency fails to create the desired distinction. Take, for example, the exposed roof structure of the bungalow-style house. Adding two nonstructural brackets to the front elevation does little. On the other hand, if the roof is designed, with large overhangs, to appear to need the brackets and they are used consistent with the historical style, the effect can be significant.

This technique would require the developer to use a larger roof overhang that appears to need or actually requires structural support. In addition, this technique creates more structure and a larger shadow line affecting the facade's appearance.

The 1950s bow window has a minor effect because it only slightly alters the plane of the facade and only at window level. When the larger bay window starts at the foundation line and has a roof detail, it is far more effective. When it protrudes over the entire story, the effect is even more dramatic. It can be carried a step further by having a bay window that extends to the second floor. Such a detail is, in fact, a minor adjustment to the floor plan because the floor area is changed.

Another trim application is the roof-wall juncture. The eaves are a place where there is an opportunity to install a variety of trim elements. This can result in a simple band of trim, several trim elements, or projecting trim that provides a more three-dimensional juncture. Likewise, gable ends can have trim elements reminiscent of various Victorian trims that provide both patterns and shadows but allow for distinctive variations. Moreover, there can be different degrees of overhangs. The gable end is also a place where material changes can have a significant effect on perspective or variety. With shingles and gable-end decoration, a great deal of variety can be created. The shingles can have very different patterns or be absent, while there can be 10 very different gable-end details, all of which result in a large number of permutations.

The presence or absence of vertical corner board trim is a common treatment used as a means of altering the facade look. Historically, wood corner details were made to look like stone corner detailing and were used in several historic styles. This type of detail can be done quite well with stucco or dri-vit, but is not readily available for use with various siding materials.

Other Architectural Features

On large houses, there are often rooms that extend three to eight feet beyond the normal plane of the facade. The larger the extension, the more the facade is broken up; however, that limits the roof-framing options available to distinguish between elevations of this floor plan. Extending the projection up past the normal roof line to mimic the attic tower room, which is found in most Victorian towers, does add distinction because the roof line is dramatically altered and maximum building height is likely to be

Figure 2-14: Roof trim is used on this small box house to create a more distinctive look.

changed. With the popularity of two-story spaces, this need not require creating a new room. Where the style approach is used, the feature must relate to the style. In the detail approach, the feature must relate in materials and detailing to the development as a whole.

In drafting regulations regarding architectural features, care should be given to assess the cost and effectiveness of each option. There is likely to be a fairly consistent relationship between the cost of the approach and its effectiveness, but creativity is important.

Figure 2-14 illustrates a very interesting, cost-effective approach altering the appearance of a small basic box. The building is a simple box with a shallow roof pitch; roof trim at the gable end and the front makes the second floor look like a large dormer on a steep roof. The result completely alters the appearance of the two-story box.

Porches

Adding or modifying porches can be another significant way to alter the facade of a house. This is true for most floor plans since the porch is, in effect, an outdoor room. It increases the depth of the house, creates a very strong shadow line, and offers a new area where detailing can change appearance. The distinction between a unit with and without a porch is clearly seen in Figure 2-15. It is also possible to look at the usefulness of the porch in altering the facade by measuring the degree to which the porch covers

Figure 2-15: There is a stark contrast between units with porches and those without.

the front elevation. Clearly, there is a difference between the simple entrance porch providing shelter from the weather while opening the front door and the full-facade porch.

One essential element is a minimum porch area. Some home builders seeking to emulate the porch mandate of New Urbanism have added a detail that looks like a porch but is too narrow for practical use. Having minimum porch areas, widths, or both is desirable. A minimum area ensures that the smallest entry-type porch at the front door has enough depth to create a distinctive feature. The minimum width forces the builder who is using a porch purely as an aesthetic device to provide enough area for it to be effective. It must be noted, however, that a porch less than three feet wide, although it can modify the facade, has no practical use.

In many cases, it is desirable to have rules permitting different porch approaches. Three types stand out as being totally different: the entrance porch, the full-facade porch, and the two-story porch. There needs to be some control on what constitutes a full-façade porch on smaller units. As the garage takes up a greater percentage of the façade, the distinction between the entrance and the full-façade porch is lost because each has a similar total area. There should be no distinction until the full façade is three times the length of the entrance façade. On wider homes, it is possible to have an intermediate porch configuration between the entrance and full-facade porches. This is a proportional analysis that can be done only by drawing different porches on a standard facade. A crude rule of thumb is that a full-facade porch should be five times the width of the entrance porch, and the intermediate porch should be one-half the width of that. In some instances, a corner porch oriented with its long side perpendicular to the street may also be successful in creating yet another porch option.

Detailing of the porch can also make a difference. A simple porch with no railings is different from one using sculpted or tooled columns with decorative railings. Eave-level detailing, as was common on Victorian houses, is another way to distinguish porches. Likewise, the use of more massive columns and railings, similar to the craftsman-type styles, can accentuate the differences between porches.

Exposed Basements

Houses with exposed basements affect building height. A typical home on a flat site has the top of the foundation only 12 inches above grade. Thus, the first-floor elevation is generally less than 24 inches above grade. If the top of the foundation is 48 inches above grade, basement windows are possible, the front door will be elevated, and the roof peak will be higher than the same model without an exposed basement (Figure 2-16). Exposing the basement does not just add space to the foundation height of the building; because roof and floor-to-floor heights have not changed, using the exposed basement approach adds three feet of height to the whole building. Raising the floor to provide basement windows also creates a more usable basement and requires the builder to provide a significant stair and entrance detail that distinguishes the building form one that sits flat on the site.

Figure 2-16: An exposed basement can raise the overall height of a unit compared to a similar unity without an exposed basement.

Modules

A module is a repetitive unit that appears in even units along a façade. Houses are often seen as having a module expressed by the window and door placement with the distance between windows centerlines being the same. This was particularly true where, historically, lining up windows on different floors was the rule. The spacing of the windows and doors and the size of the window unit can make a difference. If the house in Figure 2-

17 had a four-window module, it would have a different character with narrower, more closely spaced windows. In combination with window and door trims, window or door shape, and other details, it is possible to significantly alter the appearance of the facade by manipulating the module and the floor plan.

Windows

Fenestration (that is, the design and placement of windows) offers an opportunity to be creative in distinguishing between different elevations. The choice of double-hung or casement windows, for example, creates a very different rhythm to a facade, even if the windows are in the same location. A second option is to change the window size and grouping in a modular fashion (see above), so that there are narrower windows on the facade. Another approach is to switch from a facade with single windows in each opening to groups of two or three windows. This is a very different look, but the windows on various floors must be coordinated to prevent an unattractive, chaotic façade. Adding smaller accent windows or using French doors as windows, instead of a bank of windows, can also sufficiently alter the facade.

Historically, glass came in small panes, so mullions were used to hold the small pieces of glass in place. Today, the modern insulating glass window comes with a variety of mullion panels. This easily modified element costs almost nothing to change. The change, however, must be significant enough to be noticeable from the street. Thus, a plain glass pane with no mullions, architectural style (prairie or craftsman), and conventional panes will be noticeable, but changing the number of panes in a window is unlikely to be effective in breaking up monotony unless the mullion change is accompanied by a very different window trim package.

The use of different window trim packages or the lack of a trim package can accentuate the difference in windows. Window trim will be most important if combined with a change in fenestration pattern or window type. Again, the change needs to be easily seen from the street, so molding changes will not read unless the trim is visually much wider. Additionally, shutters are a very important element because they are highly visible from a distance, and their presence or absence is instantly noted. Furthermore, the use of decorative shapes at window heads or sills may also read well from a distance.

Entry Details

The use of different entries includes changing the number of doors, adding side lights or top lights, or providing very different trim packages. This fairly minor adjustment should be coordinated with the window treatment. It is more likely to be important on narrower units where the door and entrance hall represent a significant portion of the facade width.

Materials

A change of materials from horizontal siding to masonry or stucco will represent a significant change in appearance. Masonry is expensive, however, and attempting to use it while containing costs can lead to some of the Monopoly-set house problems discussed above. In addition, home builders might make this an optional item, causing it to become a sales burden on entry-level housing. In the past, wood was used to produce siding. Effective alternatives to clapboard types of siding were vertical siding, diagonal siding, or horizontal board siding. Unfortunately, metal, vinyl, and concrete board siding are generally available today only in the horizontal mode. Wood siding can be expensive, not just in terms of initial

Figure 2-17: *The alignment of these windows by floor and with the door on the lower floor is an example of what has since become a module.*

cost, but also in terms of maintenance, and, therefore, is not used very often.

Change to gable ends can a simple, more cost-effective material change because there is less area to be altered and thus less material required. The use of shingles or half timbers offers the potential for producing significant variety. This is most effective when there are going to be changes to style. Shingles or half timbers also can be used in different patterns that create even greater variety.

It should be noted that masonry in and of itself is not a good anti-monotony tool. Only the use of very different types of masonry prevents monotony. Stone and brick are easily distinguishable, but brick generally differs only in color. When communities require masonry in housing construction, therefore, they do not automatically reduce monotony, but they do increase the cost of housing. This can have serious consequences for housing affordability, since masonry can easily add nearly $50,000 to the cost of a unit, depending on the area of the country (labor costs are one of the greatest factors influencing this cost). The use of cast stone, thin nonstructural veneers, can reduce the cost.

In evaluating the differences between elevations of a single model, there needs to be criteria the community can use to determine whether units are sufficiently different.

Color

The early standby for creating variety in production housing was a change in color, which is not really an effective anti-monotony tool. While it is useful to have a color palette approved and to ensure changes in color, this technique should not be used as an element to increase an evaluation score. In fact, on the same model, color should be required to vary within the analysis area, and no side-by-side units, regardless of model type, should have the same color.

Garage Doors

Garage doors, generally, cannot do too much to prevent monotony; because they always look like garage doors, however, they can help. On narrow lots, the front-load garage may make up a major portion of the facade. Unfortunately, except for placing windows in the doors, it is difficult to get additional garage door options in small contemporary housing. An exception would be homes with vertical wood siding where the garage door can be designed in the same material to blend in, or in different materials to stand out. On larger garages switching from a double door to two single doors creates a different look.

EVALUATING ANTI-MONOTONY THROUGH CRITERIA

In evaluating the differences between elevations of a single model, there needs to be criteria the community can use to determine whether units are sufficiently different. Note it will also be appropriate to use the same criteria to assist in evaluating two models. The evaluation is important to ensure that styles use enough elements specific to a particular style to distinguish between them. Trivial application of style, as mentioned above, results in "neo-nothingness," where the units are not a recognizable style.

These evaluation criteria are vital to the detail approach. Only a few elements may be needed to enhance differences in style. In the case of the detail approach, nearly all the criteria will need to be used to provide a sound evaluation. This section explains the criteria. Where a control has been discussed, such as variable roof height, we will not address it again in this section, even though it may be a valuable tool. In an actual ordinance, the various controls discussed above may all be part of an evaluation or point system.

The monotony code must identify an area or block face where units are required to be different. Figure 2-18 illustrates the 10-unit block unit used to combat monotony in Lake Villa, Illinois, where no similar unit is permitted to be placed within the block. This could be reduced to a six-unit block. Facades are preapproved through the use of a point system that scores each façade, which must receive an acceptable score to be considered sufficiently different. In this format, for a pair of facades to be considered sufficiently different, one has to have a certain minimum score. If there are four elevations, they are scored against each other to determine if they meet the requisite score (see Table 2-2). Any unit that fails to meet the score will require additional design treatment or is dropped from the eligible units for that floor plan. The four design elements used in this evaluation scheme are the garage roof, the porch, roof height, roof orientation, and window treatment of four models. Contrasting the models side by side produced the score indicated in the cross-section of the row and column. Of course, other communities may decide to base the criteria on other elements, such as those listed above.

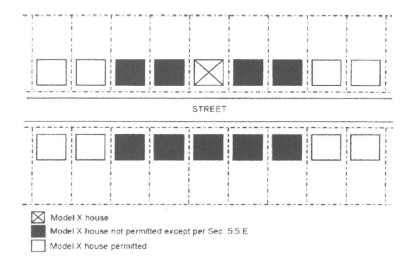

Figure 2-18: No similiar units can be placed within this 10-block area.

TABLE 2-2. SCORING MODEL 1836				
Facade	**A**	**B**	**C**	**D**
A				
B	RO, WT,GR =2.5	No match		
C	RH, P, WT, GR =3.5	P, GR, RO, WT; =3.5		
D	RH, WT, GR =2.5	P, GR, RO, WT; =3.5	P, WT =1.5 fails	

Minimum passing score 2.5 pts. Abbreviations: GR = garage roof, P=porch, RH=roof height, RO=roof orientation, WT=window treatment

Source: Lake Villa, Illinois

LOT LAYOUT AND DESIGN

Subdivision design and the configuration of lots can also assist in reducing the potential for monotony. Design and layout can be important because, while they are effective aesthetically like the changes in architectural elements discussed above, they are independent planning justifications not subject to value judgments as are the criteria for judging the effectiveness of architectural elements in preventing monotony.

Lot and Building Width

Under the standard Euclidian zoning ordinance, including most ordinances that rely on discretionary approvals, house width is highly related to lot size until lots reach estate size and proportion. In this latter case, once lots are 150 feet or more in width, which are typically lots larger than one or 1.5 acres, house width can be changed by 10 to 15 feet without problem. With such widths, distance between houses can also be varied significantly. When lots are not estate size, however, home builders seeking to create diverse floor plans have very little flexibility. Because house width is related to lot size, the models on many less-than-estate-size lots have the potential to vary by only two to four feet in width. The problem is compounded as lots become smaller. For example, detached townhouses allow no room for changing the width of the house. On small urban lots or with entry-level housing, in particular, this inflexibility severely limits the use of different floor plans to create diverse elevations.

Changes in the width of the house can be an important variable where the variation is 10 percent or more. Figure 2-19 illustrates the power of varied lot and building widths. For example, a 70-foot-wide lot would typically have houses between 51 and 54.5 feet wide. If the models range from 45 to 55 feet wide, there would be a greater potential for different room arrangements that can be reflected on the front elevation. Thus, regulations forcing the use of multiple lot widths in a block or cul-de-sac provide for very different model types, thereby reducing the potential for monotony.

There are two approaches to a variable lot configuration, both of which require the presence of two or three different widths on any block or cul-de-sac. Both should also require floor plans different for each lot-width category.

In traditional neighborhood design, windows and doors were often modular with regular spacing of windows and doors across the front elevation. One could also describe such design in terms of bays with a window or door. Thus, homes might be classified as four-, five-, six-, or seven-bay houses as illustrated in Figure 2-20. For example, a bay might be five feet wide and contain a three-foot window with a foot of siding on each side. The result is that the homes are 20, 25, 30, and 35 feet in width, respectively. The change in width, as reflected in bays, immediately sets homes apart visually, even when the architectural style is identical. Ideally, bay increments would be reflected in floor plan differences. This ap-

Changes in the width of the house can be an important variable where the variation is 10 percent or more.

Figure 2-19: The change in lot width results in a very different house in this Denver development.

proach requires homes with a window and door pattern that follows this sort of module on all floors. Highly asymmetrical window plans cannot use this system effectively.

In modern performance zoning ordinances (ordinances that use standards based on land-use intensity and the effect of a land use on other lands and facilities), varying the number and placement of bays has been used to address monotony concerns. In each housing type or lot-size category, variable lot width is mandated. Each lot-size category or housing type is based on an average lot width, with a small and large variant required. For example, a 10,000-square-foot lot might have a minimum width of 80 feet and result in a depth of 125 feet. With side yards that must total 25 feet, the maximum building width would be 55 feet. Under the regulations in a Euclidian zoning code, builders would create houses with widths of 50 to 54 feet, leaving four feet of variation. In the performance version of this example, the average lot would establish basic density and would be the same 10,000-square-foot lot. There would, however, be three lot widths and areas specified in the district. The small lot would be 70 by125 feet (8,750 square feet in area) or 12.5 percent smaller than the average lot. The large lot would be 90 by 125 feet (11,250 square feet in area) or 11.25 percent larger than the average lot. The setbacks would be identical, so that available house sizes would now range from 40 to 64 feet in width, which would allow for adjoining homes to have very different floor plans.

The performance regulations require the developer to use all three lot sizes on each block face or cul-de-sac having more than six homes. Two are required on smaller block faces or cul-de-sacs. This ensures diversity on all blocks. Along with this, the developer is required to have different model homes for each of the three types. This adds to the diversity in design and prevents the developer from grouping the three lot sizes in different parts of the subdivision. The performance ordinance sets the percentage required for the small and average lots, with the large lot being the remainder. The ordinance might require 25 percent small units and 50 percent average-size units. This is a good mix ensuring maximum diversity. It is not recommended for the minimum number of small units to be less than 15 percent of the total number of

Source: Reprinted with permission from Long and Stout 1995, 56–57

Figure 2-20: These two seven-bay houses are traditionally resigned homes on Nantucket.

units or for the average-size units to constitute more than 70 percent of all units. The same regulations can be used with the modular approach as well.

There are three planning goals the performance approach is used to achieve.

First, as discussed, it has an anti-monotony objective.

Second, it also serves the positive goal of providing a greater range of housing types and prices. It is, in fact, a strategy for affordable housing. When used to produce affordable housing, the regulations contain a maximum floor area ratio (FAR) for each size. Returning to the performance zoning ordinance example with the three lot sizes of 8,750 square feet, 10,000 square feet, and 11,250 square feet, an FAR of 0.30 would result in maximum house sizes of 2,625, 3,000, and 3,375 square feet, respectively. At $100 per square foot, this would include homes with construction cost differences of $37,500. In the total scheme of things, this is not too different from the range in prices in a conventional subdivision. If the smaller unit had a maximum FAR of 0.28, it would reduce the home to 2,450 square feet and produce a $55,000 difference. Any difference in per-square-foot costs is then magnified; a cost reduction of $5 per square foot would result in another $12,500. (The regulations intended to produce affordable housing typically also contain a requirement that exterior materials and trim be the same as those used on other units to keep the affordable units from looking cheap, even though such a requirement can increase the cost of affordable units slightly.) Obviously, the cost savings do not really become obvious until the maximum size house on the base or average lot is less than the 2,200-square-foot average house being built in the market. In the 10,000-square-foot average lot size example, therefore, an FAR of 0.22 (a 2,200-square-foot home) would be appropriate. On the small lot, a 0.20 FAR would mean a maximum house size of 1,750 square feet. The concept is carried down to all residential lot sizes and housing types so that even townhouses or apartments must be offered in a variety of sizes. In combination with other techniques, such variety can be an effective way to produce affordable units. Please note that this is not a PAS Report on affordable housing, and, consequently, we are not here addressing the other mechanisms needed to increase cost savings through the use of variable lot sizes. If a percentage of units must be affordable, smaller lots provide a means to more easily mix and disperse affordable units throughout developments. In addition, if the technique is applied to all housing types and lot sizes, it stretches the price range of market-product housing.

Finally, the variable lot provides for greater efficiency in design. In Euclidian zoning, a developer might lose lots on blocks because the property is simply a few feet too short to get in another row of lots. With the variable lots, adding an additional short lot might allow the developer to accommodate an additional lot, thus making full use of the overall site. Where properties are irregularly shaped or contain natural resource areas that require protection, there is even greater flexibility to design with the variable lot. If flexibility is the desired goal, ensure that the minimum percentage of small and average lots is provided.

Building Pads

Another way to alter the appearance and avoid monotony is to make it more difficult to assess whether two units are identical. In most Euclidian zoning ordinances, home builders build houses to the setback line. The New Urbanists carry this further, requiring buildings to be built to the setback or build-to line, which emphasizes similarities. Such an approach requires different elements to create diversity. A building pad approach would

There are three planning goals the performance approach is used to achieve. First, . . . it has an anti-monotony objective. Second, it also serves the positive goal of providing a greater range of housing types and prices. . . . Finally, the variable lot provides for greater efficiency in design.

move the building pad around on the lot, pushing it forward or back. This technique is most effective on large lots where there is a lot of room to move front to back and side to side.

Figure 2-21 shows two houses from the street and the impact of perspective, and Figure 2-22 shows the view of both houses individually. It can work on smaller lots, as well. Figure 2-23 shows what happens to two homes on small lots with very different setbacks. The photos are from a development in Mundelein, Illinois, on lots platted prior to 1950. We do not know why the home builders placed the homes with such varied setback, but it clearly creates a very different look.

As with all small-lot situations today, care must be taken to ensure that adequate room remains on the lot for patios and other elements of the modern home. On large lots, rotation of the building is also much more practical. A 30- to 45-degree rotation can produce a fairly dramatic effect, while a 90-degree rotation will generally have the same effect as having a different model on the lot.

(Top, left) **Figure 2-21:** *Variable setbacks can produce distinction in appearance;* **(below, left)** **Figure 2-22:** *The view from the road of the house on the right in Figure 2-21, which uses a deep setback;* **(below)** **Figure 2-23:** *The view from the road of the house on the left in Figure 2-21, which uses a shallow setback.*

OTHER TECHNIQUES USED TO AVOID MONOTONY
Garages

The location of the garage has changed. Alleys have gone out of favor along with the detached garage. At the turn of the twentieth century, garages were detached from the house because they functioned as part stable, part garage. The first automobile garages were also freestanding and ac-

cessed from the alley. The freestanding rear garage lasted well into the 1960s, even when there was no alley. The change in preference can be attributed to the marketing advantages of the attached garage. First, one does not have to shovel snow to reach the attached garage. Taking groceries from the car to the house is easiest in attached garages for one never needs to be exposed to inclement weather. The attached rear garage alters the usability of the rear yard, separating it from the house. Thus, the attached garage was moved to the side of the house and accessed from the front, where it became an architectural problem by reducing the availability of the facade for architectural treatment (Figures 2-24 and 2-25).

(Top) **Figure 2-24:** *The freestanding garage set in the rear of the house was a standard until well into the 1960s; (bottom)* **Figure 2-25:** *The attached garage set in the front of the house, making access to the car and the house possible without ever going outside, created an architectural problem by limiting the design options for the house facade.*

There has been a movement to return to alleys as a means of deemphasizing the automobile. It also serves as a strategy to improve general aesthetics and to combat monotony. On the smallest housing types, the front-loaded garage dominates the facade. The smaller the lot frontage and size, the more important the elimination of front-load garages becomes from an anti-monotony perspective. Today, 82 percent of the housing built has two or more car garages (U.S. Bureau of the Census 2000, C-25). Thus, any home with less than a two-car garage is more difficult to market. On the smallest freestanding homes with lots approximately 40 feet wide (essentially townhouse units with yards), if the building is 30 feet wide, the garage will take up more than 70 percent of the facade. In this example, the

Figures 2-26 and 2-27: *Compare the placement of the garage and the effect on appearance in two houses within the same subdivision. Imagine a row of houses all looking like the one on the right.*

garage door is the dominant feature of the building's architecture, and given how it overwhelms the lot, one can do very little to improve the visual impact. In townhouses, by using a T-shape common entry area where doors are recessed behind the garages, the garage can occupy up to 90 percent of the facade. From the monotony point of view, there is almost nothing to be done to cure the problem. In Figures 2-25 and 2-26, buildings in an Oswego, Illinois, subdivision with a mix of both alley and front-load garages can be compared. The homes with front-load garages are largely unaffected by the village's attempts to address monotony.

While it is clear this is more than a monotony issue, garage placement can have a tremendous impact on the effectiveness of an anti-monotony provision, particularly on smaller lots and lots with attached housing. Hence, the alley is the best choice. Alleys, however, many local governments and citizens reject the idea of alleys. Fears of crime and increased maintenance costs are just two of the reasons for their unpopularity.

Side-load, front garages. The side-load front garage (Figures 2-28 and 2-29) is a better solution where street access to the garage is desired. The side-load front garage is located in front of the house but requires drivers to make a 90-degree turn into the garage. The critical limitation on this approach is lot width. Garages typically are a minimum of 20 feet deep, and, therefore, a 55-foot lot is about the minimum required for this approach, leaving 10 feet for side yards, 45 feet for the garage, and a backing area for turning around. The great advantage of the side-load front garage is that the street elevation can be architectural and the garage can have a window treatment similar to the rest of the house. Figure 50 shows two views of the side-load front garage with a front-load garage. Landscaping can permit the side-load front garage to have a reduced setback, which is a combination of required landscaping and architectural detailing. The only regulatory issue is that the side-load garages have to alternate in direction so that people driving down the street do not see all garage doors.

Side-load garages. The side-load garage is entered from the side yard unlike the side-load front garage that is entered from the front yard. Side-load garages need a minimum of a 25- to 30-foot side yard and are, thus, available only on lots with 90 feet or more of frontage. The big advantage of this approach is that there is far more flexibility in design. The garage can be flush with the house's front facade, pushed forward, or recessed to the rear, giving the home builder three basic ways to alter the appearance of the facade with a change of plane. Like the side-load front garage, the

UNIT 500
ELEVATION A · ELEVATION B · ELEVATION C

UNIT 501
ELEVATION A · ELEVATION B · ELEVATION C

(Left) **Figure 2-28:** *Two model homes showing the variation with front-load and front side-load garages; (below)* **Figure 2-29:** *A front side-load garage on a cul-de-sac.*

orientation of the side-load garage must be changed to ensure that the garage does not dominate the view from the street. In Figure 2-30, the side-load garage is treated with architectural detail. Figure 2-31 shows a three-car side-load garage that needs landscaping to screen the garage wall. Figure 2-32 shows a well-screened side-load garage. It is also possible to move side-load garages to the rear as shown in Figure 2-33 where it can be placed behind the house and reduce the needed side yard, but this affects the available rear yard area.

(Top) **Figure 2-30:** *The side-load garage (on the right) features architectural detail on its front face. The driveway is out of the frame, off to the right; (center)* **Figure 2-31:** *This three-car-side-load garage would benefit from landscaping to screen the garage wall. When using side-load garages, they should be alternated so that a driver does not see all garage doors when coming down the street; (bottom, left)* **Figure 2-32:** *Here is effective screening of a side-load garage door; (bottom, right)* **Figure 2-33:** *These houses have side-load garages (see the door just between the houses near the center of the photo). The garage in each house is reached by a common driveway.*

Recessed front-load garages. The recessed front-load garage simply seeks to use perspective and shadowing to camouflage the fact the garage is taking up a sizable portion of the front facade. The garage should be located a minimum of 20 feet behind the front elevation of the house and more if the unit has a porch front. Typically, the lots would be a minimum of 60 to 65 feet wide for a two-car recessed front-load garage, with a minimum 20- to 25-foot setback (Figure 2-34).

Mews. The mews is a pedestrian street with no automobile access, where vehicular access is from an alley. Houses front the mews with the rear of the house oriented to the alley, as shown in Figure 2-35. Most people approach the units on foot through the mews, resulting in a house that faces open space and provides a safe space for children to play. Even if the homes on opposite sides of a mews are no further apart than if they faced a street, a much more attractive setting is provided (Figure 2-36). The street views are side yards of only a fraction of the total units, so the monotony problem is reduced in scale, and landscaping of the mews helps break up views of other units.

The mews represents a way to address two issues about the use of alleys. First, local governments often resist the alley due to increased maintenance costs. The mews reduces these costs by lowering street maintenance costs. Second, some home builders object to the use of alleys because, unless they get concessions on the street widths, the infrastructure costs of

Figure 2-34: A recessed front-load garage.

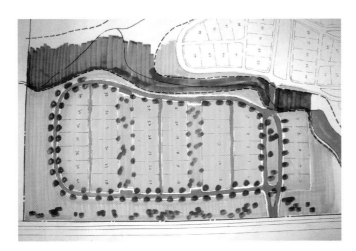

Figures 2-35 and 2-36: Mews are pedestrian streets with no automobile access. All access is through alleys. There are a number of benefits to using the mews approach, including safety for residents and savings in infrastructure costs.

development increase. Again, the use of mews reduces infrastructure costs for the developer as well as the body responsibility for street maintenance.

Landscaping

The changes in landscape design over the last 100 years have transformed housing, particularly in suburban settings. It was common in early suburban and even some urban settings for the lot to be surrounded by hedges. In the suburbs, these hedges were often six or more feet in height and, in some cases, were hedgerows containing shrubs, and canopy and understory trees.

Today, the production house comes with minimal landscaping, the majority of which is concentrated on the foundation line, to serve as accents to the house, rather than as a yard enclosure. Figures 2-37 and 2-38 illustrate the accent approach.

As any observer of community preference surveys can attest, with all other things being equal, slides showing the presence of mature vegetation leads to a higher level of satisfaction among survey participants. This occurs because screening breaks the building mass by interposing a vegetative mass and creating distinctive identities (as well as the natural beauty of the landscaping itself). People respond positively to trees that are taller than the house and that shelter the building (Figure 2-38).

(Left) **Figure 2-37:** *Landscaping used as an accent to the house, rather than as a way of defining the yard; (right)* **Figure 2-38:** *Perimeter landscaping, especially with landscaping of sufficient variety and height, can break up the mass of a building, helping to create diversity and distinction between similar houses.*

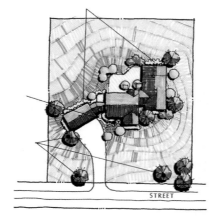
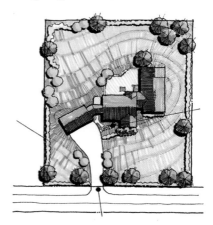

Site Grading

Production housing usually begins by mass grading the site, whereby both existing vegetation and topography are destroyed. Most engineers argue that, for smaller lots, they have to mass grade the site due to concerns about drainage and driveway slopes.

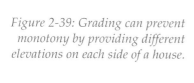

Figure 2-39: Grading can prevent monotony by providing different elevations on each side of a house.

Figure 2-40: This lot is higher than the ones around it, using grading to achieve differentiation within the block.

In earlier times, there was more flexibility in grading the site. There are examples of streets with a different elevation on each side (Figure 2-39). Increasing the height of the lot with respect to its neighbors alters the average lot line. A short stretch of street could have a slight cut, resulting in a few lots being higher (Figure 2-40). The difference can be relatively modest (Figure 2-41) or extreme (Figure 2-42).

Figures 2-41 and 2-42: Grading can creat modest effects (below, left) or dramatic ones (below, right).

In extreme situations, alley access may be needed; however, with moderate differences, there should be no problem with driveway slopes. Front-load garages may need to be further back than the normal setback line, but that is consistent with better design, in any case.

CHAPTER 3

Monopoly-Set Houses

roduction housing seeks to cut costs at every turn by providing the maximum volume for the lowest cost. This is a recent trend because in the 1950s homes were smaller and relied on small compact rooms. The result of the current trend is the bean counters eliminate the details that make buildings interesting. Prior to World War II, lower-price housing usually meant smaller homes, but the small home builder followed basic styles on small and large homes alike. Nowadays, the production builder has increased volume and size, as well as decreased costs, as goals. Modern materials have changed the way homes are built, and the relentless drive to trim costs has created the Monopoly-set house. Too frequently, homes over the last two decades look remarkably similar to this simplistic plastic shape. The result is, simply put, unattractive (Figure 3-1). There are three major elements that characterize the Monopoly-set house: roof-wall juncture, modern siding and windows, and false fronts.

Figure 3-1: *It doesn't take much imagination to see these houses as very similar to those used in a Monopoly set, although they are closer to the "hotel" unit than the "house" unit.*

The juncture of the roof and walls is an integral part of the structural frame, and in traditional housing also provided a location for many details that added interest to the building. Detailing at the eaves added visual interest and created a shadow line, which is a visible and changing element of the building's appearance. The overhang of the roof, eaves, and detailing all add costs to the house; the result is that, on the gable end, the overhang has been totally eliminated in favor of a single trim board with no overhang. Gutters are the only overhang remaining and are inadequate to produce a good shadow line.

The advent of metal and vinyl siding and modern-clad or metal windows has stripped houses of more possibilities for detailing. In wood construction, for example, framing details provided interest, as well as making the home weatherproof. The modern materials reduce these joints to trivial dimensions and create the appearance of windows in the siding that look as if they were created by a punch press.

Builders have attempted to provide some relief from the stripped down box by dressing up the front elevation with trim and other features. This provides some street appeal. But it is clearly false because the sides are exposed to view. For neighbors to the rear there is no relief to the basic box.

In addition to these three major elements, Monopoly-set housing often suffers from insufficient landscaping that exposes the plainness of the homes. As a tool to combat this, street trees should be an absolute minimum requirement in all developments. The landscaping problems mentioned under the monotony section also apply to the Monopoly-set house issue.

ROOF-WALL JUNCTURES

Overhanging eaves can be mandated. The minimum overhang should be at least 12 inches to provide a good shadow line. Many historic housing types had even more pronounced overhangs (Figure 3-2). A regulation requiring a minimum overhang is one solution. The shadow line created by the overhang is enough to provide some interest at the roof-wall plane. Ideally, the home builders would also use trim to provide additional interest at this juncture. The combination of trim and shadow line provides a richer visual experience.

The minimum overhang is a simple regulation. It can, however, produce monotony. There was a time when houses often sought to replicate some style, but with the exception of New Urbanist developments, contemporary homes have, by and large, given up any attempt at style, either modern or historic. Historic styles had varying degrees of overhangs, with the largest—three feet or more—found on the prairie, craftsman, and bungalow styles. The Cape Cod and other similar early English-style homes had no significant overhang. Minimum overhang ordinances should be written to require home builders to use a variety of overhangs. The regulations could provide a minimum and a higher average overhang. An option should be available for builders to have overhangs and trim details true to the historic styles.

MODERN SIDING AND WINDOWS

Windows and trim were, historically, a major feature of architecture. The advent of modern windows and vinyl- and metal-sided homes eliminated most of the constraints governing traditional window construction and detailing. Wood siding is disappearing, and nearly all new siding materials are made to look like lapboard or clapboard wood siding. Today, metal or metal-clad windows come with a nailing strip and are installed before the siding. The siding laps over the nailing tab, providing only a thin line of trim less than an inch wide. The slightly sawtoothed texture, when combined with the narrow window trim and near-flush wall mounting, creates the punch-out appearance (Figure 3-3). It was not a problem with older wood construction because the trim was essential to making the window functional and keeping water out. Figure 3-4 illustrates a simple wood-framing window detail. While trim packages are available, as shown in Figure 3-5, they are not used on many entry-level housing developments. In masonry buildings, the positioning of the window back from the wall plane mitigates the impact of the narrower window trim elements because there is a shadow line.

While mandating some trim is one solution, it is not recommended, except where there is no willingness to adopt a monotony code. Monotony codes require attention to trim packages but also encourage creativity to distinguish units of the same type. Regulations addressing the false front will also address the trim problem, except in the lowest-cost housing where there may be no false-front options.

Figure 3-2: This overhange creates visual interest at the roof-wall plane, a feature missing in most modern housing.

There is a secondary window problem that has evolved in recent years: the random window. In nearly all historical styles (the modern and international styles are major exceptions), there was some rationality to window placement, setting up a modular or bay appearance. Typically, windows shared the same head elevation and were often the same size around the building or on any one facade. As can be seen in Figures 3-6 and 3-7, the random window treatment is fairly common. Similarly, elevations with only a few windows have become more common. The punched-out window on nearly plain walls creates an eyesore. It used to be that windows were important on all outside walls.

(Left) Figure 3-3: The punch-out window; (center) Figure 3-4: Wooden trim can create more visual interest to the typical punch-out window; (right) Figure 3-5: An added trim package. It's the details that can make a difference; compare these windows with the one shown in Figure 3-3.

Figure 3-6: The blank wall, offering no rhyme or reason for window placement.

Figure 3-7: Windows placed randomly and without regard to uniformity in size on a house's side wall.

FALSE FRONTS

The false front is a common home builder's response to the monotony problem. Adding trim to the front elevation, which can be varied from unit to unit, helps distinguish units from each other. In Figure 3-8, the front of the house has been provided with window trim and the facade dressed up. The rear view of the same house (Figure 3-9) exposes a very different and unattractive view. This problem is not limited to starter houses. Figures 3-10 and 3-11 show a house with a well-designed front, aligned windows, highly detailed brick trim, and small dormers. It all falls apart on the side, however, where there is no apparent effort to distinguish the façade. This problem has several solutions. The first and simplest is to require 360-degree treatment of window, door, and corner trim detailing. Even on a very simple house, window trim consistency, as shown in Figure 3-12, goes a long way to eliminating the problem. Thus, if shutters are applied to the windows on the front of the house, the shutters must be carried around to side and rear elevations. For most markets, the developer has a vested interest in providing some diversity in housing. Requiring the application of trim packages on all elevations will address both the false-front problem and the punched-out window problem.

Figures 3-8 and 3-9: The same house from front and back. The front uses window trim and facade elements to try to provide distinction, but the side and rear are blank. Again, note the absence of landscaping, so that the disappointing contrast between front, side, and rear is in plain view.

Figures 3-10 and 3-11: The effort spent on detailing the front of this house (left) is lost with the "snout" garage and the failure to wrap features of the detailing around the side.

Figure 3-12: Here, the detailing is kept consistent from front to side, the roof overhang works, and the garage does not interfere with the facade.

The second level of control is to require materials, as well as trim, to be carried around to all sides of the building (Figure 3-13). The masonry veneer applied to many home fronts appears simulated since the single brick depth is visible and apparent to anybody walking or driving down the street (Figure 3-14). The recent advent of two-inch veneers that are glued in place reduces costs but makes the corner treatment more important. The same holds true for other materials applied to the front, such as faux Tudor trim.

The 360-degree material treatment requirement works on all false-front materials. For masonry, there is a substantial cost issue with 360-degree regulations. Historically, whether the house was wood or masonry, the materials were used on all facades. Today, this is a cost issue for home builders, particularly with masonry since it is more labor intensive than siding or trim details.

Figure 3-13: Use of the front facade materials around a building should be mandatory.

Figure 3-14: The false brick front is obvious to any viewer, especially when seen from the side. Also note the elements not carried around to the side (e.g., shutters, trim).

The cost issue need not preclude the use of the 360-degree standard for masonry. On a two-story house, full masonry can easily add $50,000 to a house price. Increased cost is an issue because home builders need to have options that buyers will use, and until you get to luxury homes, 360-degree masonry is unaffordable. All masonry homes are going to be more expensive, which raises a concern about it being an exclusionary technique. With a small building (for example, one that is 30 feet in the front and 20 feet deep), the cost of the false front would be only 30 percent of that of the 360-degree, two-story masonry application (see Table 3-1). There is no mandate that masonry needs to be two stories high. Applying masonry only to the first floor level (Figure 3-15) cuts the cost of masonry by more than half

TABLE 3. COST COMPARISON OF DIFFERENT MASONRY APPLICATIONS

Masonry Application	Total Area Covered by Masonry	Percent of Masonry Cost
360-Degree Masonry	1,404 sq. ft.	100
False Front (Full Masonry)	420 sq. ft.	30
360-Degree Masonry to Second Floor	776 sq. ft.	55
360-Degree Masonry to bottom of First-Floor Windows	300 sq. ft.	21
360-Degree Masonry of basement (two ft.)	200 sq. ft.	14

This analysis is based on a two-story, hipped-roof house. Masonry to the side gable end would add 100 square feet of masonry.

(Top) **Figure 3-15:** *Masonry need not be applied to both stories of the house, keeping cost under control while providing visual interest; (below)* **Figure 3-16:** *A brick "return." A rule of thumb might be a minimum of 24 inches or three, eight-inch brick lengths to make the return visually significat enough to warrant its use.*

Masonry can be applied to the window sills or to the first-floor level line, which is less costly than a two-story false front. Thus, there are three intermediate 360-degree masonry applications with historical antecedents available for consideration. Additionally the two-inch masonry veneer is less expensive, allowing for more coverage at a given cost.

Another approach to the front facade is to require masonry to be applied around the corner, either to the first break in plane or to a set distance (called a return). Where there is a change in plane on side elevations, the change-of-plane standard is most effective because of its natural look. This will not work on boxlike houses since there are no changes in plane. An alternative is to require a minimum return. Bricks are generally four by eight inches (width and length); one-and-a-half bricks represent a 12-inch return. The greater the return, the more substantial the false front appears. A three-brick return of 24 inches is a good minimum (Figure 3-16).

Many contemporary houses add three dimensions to the front facade to provide greater interest and to combat monotony. Another way to use masonry is to apply it to only a three-dimensional facade element. It is not uncommon for additions or wings of buildings to consist of different materials than the main structure, as can be seen in Figure 3-15. This illustration also shows masonry up to the second-floor level. This is a natural looking way to apply materials because all four sides of the original structure are clad in masonry. This approach works with all material applications, but it requires a floor plan with enough articulation to create one or more wings on the house (Figure 3-17).

Figure 3-17: *With a floor plan that produces wings on the house, whole wings can differ in the application of materials, giving a varied, distinctive overall look.*

CHAPTER 4

The Too-Big House

Simply stated, the "too-big house" is one too big for the lot on which it sits. The community may believe these houses are out of scale with the rest of the community or may feel they create an undesirable character. Our modern society is currently on a bigness binge in homes and cars (witness the success of the Hummer, a vehicle essentially too big for our road and parking systems). As discussed in previous chapters, home size is increasing. It can be said that virtually every aspect of the modern home is being enlarged—from storage space (contrast the storage in a modern house with that of a craftsman-style home of the early twentieth century) to room size. Ironically, the number of bedrooms is increasing as family size is declining, a trend that is also found in car ownership, which also results in an increase in the average garage size.

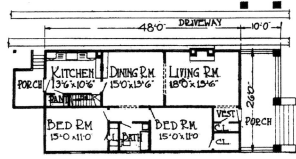

Figure 4-1: This Craftsman-style home is actually narrow but uses the porte-cochére to make it look wider. Note the size of the rooms. Smaller can be beautiful.

Size has clearly become the standard, and, as a result, quality has declined across nearly all housing markets. Only in very high-end housing does there seem to be much interest in quality, and that is only in the cost of the materials. The attention to craftsmanship in house construction is almost nonexistent. In suburban and some urban settings, the dominant theme seems to be to create a house that appears very large from the curb— a statement of wealth and conspicuous consumption.

The underlying issue is the way we design buildings. In part, this is seen in the modern floor plan, which provides more rooms with less usability, such as more bedrooms than family size dictates, master suites bigger than 1950s homes, etc. In addition, "vacant volume," vaulted ceilings, two-story spaces, and taller ceilings are all symptoms of the problem. The ego booster, the mandatory two-story entry hall and living room, has become a status symbol.

The too-big house is a problem in many communities and neighborhoods. On smaller lots, homes built to the setback lines in every direction are recent phenomena. They create problems for zoning because most ordinances do not permit the other major status symbol, the "deck," to intrude into the yard. Thus, the too-big house creates demands for variances for intrusions into the side or rear yard because neither the house purchaser nor the developer was smart enough to provide these spaces within the setback lines. For the community, the too-big house may simply draw too much attention to it, particularly when built in open land, or it may be seen as representing a general change in community character.

The increased height of vacant volume, such as the cathedral ceiling, is driving up overall heights dramatically, even when floor area is not changing. Modern windows and insulation also contribute to making these spaces possible. The increased height makes the new subdivisions or housing appear out of context with housing built on the same lots 20 to 50 years ago. In either urban neighborhoods or suburban greenfield subdivisions, compared to the historical pattern of development in the community, the homes appear much larger and seem to overwhelm the lot. Consequently, the new homes look to have a different character, due to their scale in relationship to the lot.

For decades, a two-story house existed well within a 35-foot height limit. With a floor 1.5 feet above grade and the ceiling of the second floor less than 20 feet up, even the steeply pitched roofs of the Tudor style with a front gable orientation could be accommodated. Turning to a side gable end, increasing house size, adding walk out or English basements, and going to 10- or 12-foot ceilings has pushed the height as high as 42 to 43 feet. At these heights, shear bulk becomes a problem. In the suburbs, building mass dominates the street face, creating enclosed architectural space where previously there was a balance between garden and building that helped shape the desired character. In urban neighborhoods, architectural context is ignored, and the house looks completely out of place.

While the problem has other roots, zoning only has the tools to regulate the symptoms, rather than the cause. There are a number of approaches to regulating bulk that can be introduced into zoning and land development codes.

BULK REGULATION STANDARDS

There are six tools planners can use to regulate bulk: lot setbacks, building coverage, floor area ratios, height, building volume ratios, and landscape volume ratio. These tools will be explored in this section. The building volume ratio is the best of these measures, while all the other bulk regulations are approximations.

Lot Setbacks

Lot setbacks are the original zoning control for bulk; they prevent the building from occupying more than a certain percentage of the lot. This is a relatively crude measure, however, since it is only a two-dimensional standard and ignores height. With the exception of small urban lots, nobody traditionally thought much about this standard. In most jurisdictions, the setback easily accommodated the house and various elements, such as decks and rear garages. Only in the last 20 years has there been a trend toward homes that occupy the full area created by the setback lines. As a result, nobody is evaluating what a building that fills the building pad will look like in comparison to its neighbors on similar lots. A lot that was gracious in 1950, when the average home was 983 square feet, may not graciously accept a 2,265-square-foot average house size (the average size in the year 2000).

As an example, a 7,500-square-foot lot with typical setbacks (the lot is 70 feet by 100 feet with a 25-foot front yard, a 30-foot rear yard, and a total of 20 feet of side yard(s)) results in a buildable area within the setbacks of 2,475 square feet. This is approximately 2.5 times the floor area of the average home in 1950, including the ranch house. Today, that same lot will barely accommodate a 2,400-square-foot ranch home. Hence, setbacks do an excellent job of controlling how close two buildings may be, but they do little to address bulk. One thought is that they can be modified to maintain the building setback or pad size. This requires the planner to evaluate the type of house that can be built within the setbacks and increase the setbacks to limit house size. Another approach that also needs to be considered is whether decks should be permitted in the yards to eliminate the need for variances when the house fills the area within the setback.

Building Coverage

Some communities recognize the limitations of setbacks by adding a building coverage requirement, which is the percentage or ratio of the building coverage to the lot area (Figure 4-2). A 10,000-square-foot lot might have a building pad inside the setback line of 3,850 square feet (assuming a lot 80 feet by 125 feet with a minimum 25-foot front yard, a 30-foot rear years, and a minimum total of 25 feet of side yard(s)). A two-story home occupying the entire building pad would be 7,700 square feet, an enormous size by any standard. A building coverage ratio determines how much of a site may be covered by the dwelling. The building coverage ratio is the area covered by the building divided by lot area. Thus, on the 10,000-square-foot lot, a building coverage ratio of 0.20 limits buildings to 20 percent of the lot area, 2,000 square feet, or 53 percent of the building pad. Thus, a two-story house could reach a maximum size of 4,000 square feet, a sub-

Setbacks do an excellent job of controlling how close two buildings may be, but they do little to address bulk.

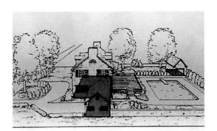

Figure 4-2. *The concept of Building Coverage (BC).*

stantial reduction from 7,700 square feet. Further, there would be 1,800 square feet available for decks or other areas within the setback lines. The principal problem with building coverage as a standard is that it totally fails to deal with the vertical, the third dimension. A building coverage set when ranch homes were the standard is apt to permit a vastly oversize two-story unit. On the other hand, too tight of a limit might prohibit ranch-style homes.

Floor Area Ratio (FAR)

A great many communities have replaced building coverage regulations with FAR. FAR is the ratio of total building floor area to the area of the site (Figure 4-3). Unlike building coverage, FAR takes multiple floors into account. Thus it uses floors as a surrogate for height. Figures 4-4 and 4-5 illustrate two buildings with similar lots and building coverages, but very different FARs.

In general, FAR is a better measure of bulk. Nevertheless, floor area is still a surrogate that provides some idea about bulk but can never be completely accurate. The greatest inaccuracies are likely to occur in non-residential structures where building heights can vary quite significantly (the one-story office building with a height of 15 to 18 feet versus a warehouse with 50-foot heights). With residential structures, the differ-

(Above, left) **Figure 4-3:** *Floor Area Ratio; (right)* **Figures 4-4 and 4-5:** *Two houses with on similar-size lots with similar building coverage, but with very different FARs.*

ences are not likely to be so dramatic, but serious problems do occur. One problem is how to count basements. On a flat site, basements are underground and do not contribute to building volume. However, lookout basements (that is, basements partially aboveground with windows but no doors) add substantial building volume to the house. A set of rules is needed to address how to count floor area for all types of basements including those that are below ground. Similarly, cathedral ceiling, two-story spaces, and attic space also cause problems by creating substantial volumes over and above what would be anticipated from the floor-area measurements.

Thus, while it is possible to create a series of rules to measure floor area(for example, some ordinances require any space with a ceiling higher than 12 feet or some other figure to be counted as two stories), such rules are difficult to write clearly and broadly enough to deal with the variety of possible physical conditions.

Height

Height measures building bulk in only one dimension and is an essential addition to the various two-dimensional standards. It is important to note the definition of height is a critical issue. No matter what the definition, with pitched roofs, the chance is the total volume of the house will be inaccurately measured. The following is a short review of different aspects of height. Note that a number of these factors may be combined in an ordinance definition.

- Height above grade. A very constraining definition that measures the maximum height from lowest point on the site.

- Height above average grade. This adds to the building height on sloped sites.

- Height above natural grade. This seeks to prevent filling of sites to provide walkout basements.

- Height to roof peak. This measures the highest point on the building.

- Height to midpoint of pitched roof. This attempts to get at volume by allowing a building with a pitched roof to be taller than one with a flat roof.

The midpoint definition accurately accounts for a gabled roof; however, it overestimates hipped roofs. If there are dormers, the result will be an underestimation of volume. The basement problem carries over to heights, particularly where the site is sloped.

Grade is another issue that creates problems for the measurement of height. Ideally, the measurement used is the finished grade of the house, which means measuring the average grade around the building. Some sort of limitation on altering grade may be needed to avoid berming to mask the real height.

Building Volume Ratio (BVR)

The BVR is a true volume indicator that requires measuring the entire volume of the building above finished grade, or the visible portion of the building (Figure 4-6). Basements, attics, cathedral ceilings, and higher floor-to-ceiling heights are all accounted for by BVR. The building volume ratio is as follows:

$$BVR = BV/10/LA$$
Where BV is building volume and LA is lot area

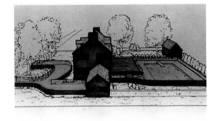

Figure 4-6: Building Volume Ratio (BVR)

While many people think the calculation is very difficult, the reality is that with the widespread use of computer-aided design (CAD) systems by architects and architectural firms that produce plans for production builders, it is not much more difficult than working through the floor area rules for most production housing. Further, one may find that the building inspector is already doing most of these calculations. For example, the inspector may be checking floor area calculations for permit fees and reporting them to the assessor's office. In addition, some are using building volume to get a better handle on the total construction costs in order to maximize building permit revenue. The calculation should be required of the architect or designer and sealed to ensure accuracy. This is the best measure of building volume or bulk. It is the only three-dimensional measure and is highly recommended.

One additional benefit to the BVR is that architects or builders can manipulate the house plan to maximize floor area or any other housing attribute within the maximum BVR. Lower roof pitches lower total volume, thus permitting additional floor area if that is the goal. Likewise, grand spaces with high ceilings can be provided, resulting in lower floor areas. The BVR is not tied to any single element (floor area or ground coverage) and, thus, provides maximum flexibility for the designer to achieve their most important elements.

Landscape Volume Ratio (LVR)

Landscaping has been shown to be effective in controlling monotony and the Monopoly-set house. Landscape volume is similar to the building volume, except that it measures the volume of the landscape material (Figure 4-7). The landscape volume is calculated as follows

$$LSR = LSV/10/LA$$

Where BV is building volume and LA is lot area

The landscape volume can achieve several things: it can shelter the building where trees are taller than the buildings, can screen buildings, and can provide camouflage as illustrated in Figure 4-8. The result is a softening of the impact of the building. The concern with the barren look of new subdivisions with very small trees is recognizes this problem.

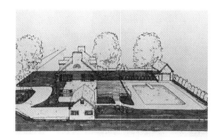

(Above) **Figure 4-7:** *Landscape Volume Ratio;* (right) **Figure 4-8:** *Landscaping can screen bulk to diminish the effect of the too-big house.*

THE "NOT-SO-BIG HOUSE"

The root of the problem exemplified by the "too big house" is America's romance with size, which is a recurring theme in American architectural history. While the craftsman school of architecture at the end of the nineteenth century was a response to the crude nature of many mass-produced products, critiques of the current American fascination with the too-big house have arisen. (The best example is Sarah Susanka's *The Not So Big House Collection* (Taunton Press 2002), which includes two of the books she's written on the concept.)

A look at homes from the early part of the twentieth century finds compact floor plans, including small kitchens and reasonably proportioned master suites and closets. Similarly, bathrooms, whose numbers have also increased, typically went into a 50-square-foot space and now routinely exceed 100 square feet. While status fuels the desire for multistory spaces for living rooms, master bedrooms, and halls, none of these things are really related to the quality or even to the cost of the house. Craftsmanship and careful design can create more attractive rooms, more livable spaces, and show that care and design went into the building.

Work needs to be done to get the press, home builders, and the building industry in general to encourage higher-quality housing for all price levels. The cycle of bigger is better needs to be broken, and education is essential in this. It is not uncommon to hear complaints of how cheap, entry-level housing is a rationale against small lots or attached housing. Unfortunately, the same mentality is found in McMansions and starter castles. Instead of building rooms with higher ceilings and two-story spaces, the money could be better used in quality materials, detailing, and architecture designed to accommodate the family's needs, rather than perpetuate the ostentatious display of wealth. A more discerning approach would be to recognize the quality of the design or at least quality materials. Figures 4-9 and 4-10 represent several homes designed as "not-so-big houses."

Source: Reprinted with permission from Susanka 2000, p.104

Figure 4-9: Affordable Comfort.

Work needs to be done to get the press, home builders, and the building industry in general to encourage higher-quality housing for all price levels.

Adrian Fine, National Trust for Historic Preservation

Figure 4-10: Compared to the "affordable comfort" of the above "not-so-big" house, this monster home on an infill lot overwhelms its neighborhood, screaming "look at me, look at me."

CHAPTER 5

Teardowns

Teardowns are a special case of the too-big house.

Simply put, a teardown involves destroying an existing structure to build another. In some cases, it involves a massive addition to an existing house. The major difference between teardowns and the too-big house is that the teardown occurs in an existing neighborhood, where the too-big house is usually new (a greenfield addition) out of scale with its neighbors. In some cases, the teardown results in a massive building closer to the neighbor than the unit that was originally there.

Figure 5-1. In some cases, teardowns are not a bad thing. Here, a home like the one on the left may provide a needed upgrade to a neighorhood's image. But planners must be careful to make sure that an adequate supply of affordable housing remains so as to not displace those citizens and community workers who rely on such housing.

From a regulatory perspective, the difference is that the economics leading to a teardown have social issues unrelated to design. Some of these are common with gentrification issues. Teardowns often occur in neighborhoods where the housing stock is sound, but dated, and where the character of the neighborhood has been considered desirable for some time. A variation of the teardown can occur in neighborhoods where the housing is deteriorated. In these areas replacement is desirable except when the buildings have significant historic value. Indeed, many deteriorating neighborhoods would benefit from teardowns.

Because it occurs on an existing lot with a house, obsolescence is an important distinction between the too-big house and the teardown. Existing houses in a neighborhood may typically be a minimum of 30 to 50 years old. The bathrooms, kitchens, bedrooms, and storage areas are too small for modern tastes. The styles and colors, equipment, and materials are also dated. Further, there is likely a need to refurbish and repair many little problems in the house accumulated through age: cracks, inadequate electrical systems, heating, air conditioning, plumbing, and general restoration. Additionally, there may be, in some instances, structural problems; however, this is not likely to be a contributing factor in most neighborhoods threatened with teardowns unless they fell out of favor and are not thought to be up and coming. Consequently, this creates a situation where the home is out of sync with the perceived needs of the individuals interested in purchasing the property—the perfect setting for a teardown *and* a too-big house.

ECONOMICS DRIVE TEARDOWNS

Economics is the issue that makes the teardown very different from the too-big house. A lot with a potential teardown has a very high land value relative to the existing house. For new housing, the generalized real estate rule is the lot should be no more than 25 percent of the total value of the property. This will not necessarily remain constant over time. For teardowns, the lot is likely to be 50 percent or more of the value of the entire property, and in many cases, the land value will exceed the value of the house. If one can buy a vacant lot with similar locational values, there is no sense in spending substantially more for a teardown lot. The market must support the teardown as a rational investment. The total cost of the new house includes the lot, the initial house, the demolition costs, and the cost of the new house.

The unique economics also contribute to the problem because of the impact on neighbors. As land values inflate and taxes rise, a condition accelerated by teardowns, pressure is put on the existing residents who may have moved into the neighborhood many years ago. As a result, many who oppose the teardowns may feel they are being taxed out of their homes and neighborhoods. Another group of residents may look at the increase as an opportunity to profit and move up to more modern homes. These political issues simultaneously make it more difficult to reach consensus about what should be done to address what some see as a problem and others see as a right and opportunity.

Neighborhoods with well-established community character reflect that character through lot size, house size, height, and vegetation. In a new sub-division, all the homes will share the too-big house classification, so, while the community as a whole may react negatively, no resident is threatened by the too-big unit next door, as is the case with a teardown. In existing neighborhoods, the teardown alters the character of the neighborhood. For planners, this alteration of the existing character, in combination with the economics, makes the problem far more difficult to address.

Another perspective on the teardown is that it potentially represents mass gentrification of the neighborhood, which is a real threat to affordable housing in the community. The most vulnerable neighborhoods in the community will be the ones where housing costs are the lowest because the market considers the neighborhood desirable but the dwellings not in keeping with modern tastes. A loss of a neighborhood to teardowns and to gentrification reduces the community's ability to ensure the availability of housing for municipal employees, service workers, or other blue-collar workers.

A local government that does nothing about the too-big house does not necessarily create problems for the majority of its residents. The community is likely to have a very high income and status. Most community residents are happy with increasing status and property values. Unless the neighborhood has historic value, the sad fact is that a reduced supply of more affordable housing and increased difficulty for municipal employees to live in a community may note be a high priority. The exception to this is the resort community where tourism and housing for workers is a problem for the business community and the wages they pay.

PREDICTING TEARDOWNS

Predicting and addressing the problem before a teardown "crisis" begins is essential. Teardowns, as discussed above, are all about market. The neighborhood subject to teardowns is a highly desirable one. Thus, following market trends will be especially helpful in early identification of a teardown problem. In larger cities, neighborhoods must be studied for signs of changing economics, while in the suburbs, the whole community is likely to exhibit the changes. Access to public transportation, waterfront, and/or recreational opportunities and tourism are perhaps other factors driving the economics.

It is important to note teardowns are typically found in those communities where current new house sizes are well above the national average. Monitoring census data about the community and comparing it to averages within the region will also be a clue as to the potential for teardowns. A community showing increases in average incomes exceeding those of its neighbors over the same period of time will have greater potential for teardowns.

There is some predictability in determining where teardowns will become a problem. First, they will occur in neighborhoods where the standard unit is among the smallest in the community. Depression era homes, as well as homes from the late 1940s through the 1950s, are particularly vulnerable. The 900- to 1,400-square-foot house is clearly vulnerable since these are close to half the size of the average house in 2000. A second indicator of vulnerability is the number of stories. Ranch houses will be vulnerable in an era when two-story homes are the standard. Similarly, the split-level, which was popular in some parts of the country, is also a vulnerable housing format. Thus, a planner can identify neighborhoods with homes vulnerable to teardowns simply by driving around town.

Once planners identify neighborhoods as prime candidates for teardowns, they should look for a gap between neighborhood house size and zoning district regulations. This can be found by comparing the average house size and footprint with the building pad defined by the setbacks. On small lots, anywhere that the house footprint is less than 60 percent of the building pad, teardowns or major reconstruction with the same net impact are likely.

If a community can identify neighborhoods at risk before problems arise, solutions will be much easier. Regulations are far easier to revise when the regulations do not create a burden for buyers or people who want to upgrade the home. Aside from the political issue, it would be better to plan for redevelopment and have a strategy in place before the market begins to dictate teardowns.

REGULATING TEARDOWNS

The same regulations used for the too-big house apply here: setbacks, building coverage, floor area ratio, height, and building volume ratio. In looking at these same indicators again for teardowns, we will focus on what can be done in each case. Recognizing the realities of obsolescence and small size, it is important to base planning on recognition of the need for some home expansion. Prohibiting any expansion is undesirable, as this will ultimately lead to disinvestment as owners became frustrated with the ability to adapt the units to modern needs.

Once a neighborhood is identified as being at risk for teardowns, the first objective should be to work out reasonable expansion plans to permit modernization and reasonable expansion without destroying neighborhood character. An example of this type of analysis can be found in Avi Friedman's *Planning the New Suburbia* (University of British Columbia Press, 2001), which discusses and illustrates this type of analysis in Canadian cities. Figures 5-2 and 5-3 illustrate the concept.

Ideally, the regulations allow normal upgrading of the neighborhood to retain vitality without permitting the too-big house, which turns the neighborhood over to another economic class. A complete study would look at typical floor plans of the dominant housing in the neighborhood and think through expansion strategies related to the floor plans in order to provide guidance to the homeowners. Such a study is best carried out by architects because they will be able to deal with floor plan revisions. The planner and architect then need to work together to evaluate all the zoning standards. Having both architectural, lot layout, and design concepts available can educate the community and builders. There may be a shortcut available. If there has been a history of contextual additions in the neighborhood, they should be reviewed to determine if they represent a sound basis for regulations. Once planners can create some estimate of the extent and nature of suitable extensions, they can draft regulations. (See also pages 49-52 above.)

Setbacks

When setbacks are such that they allow a major expansion of building size, they should be increased to reduce the pod. The goal should be to allow a

Once planners identify neighborhoods as prime candidates for teardowns, they should look for a gap between neighborhood house size and zoning district regulations.

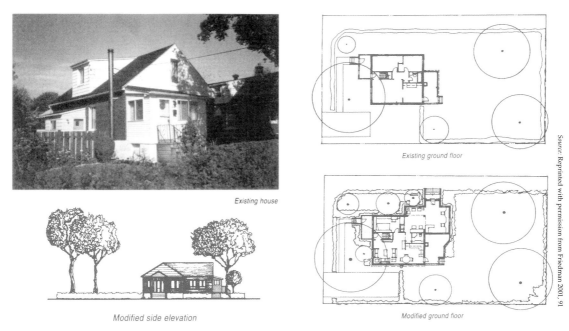

Existing house

Modified side elevation

Existing ground floor

Modified ground floor

Source: Reprinted with permission from Friedman 2001, 91

Figure 5-2: *To accommodate the opening of a neighborhood business, a beauty salon, an addition was made to an existing unit. In addition, the second floor was developed as a home office and recreation room.*

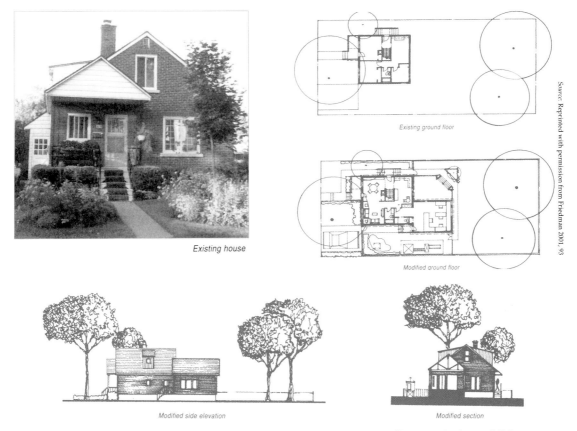

Existing house

Existing ground floor

Modified ground floor

Modified side elevation

Modified section

Source: Reprinted with permission from Friedman 2001, 93

Figure 5-3: *The creation of another local business, a desktop publishing office, required an addition to the rear of a unit. A separate entrance was needed, and the space of the exisiting unit was reorganized. A new recreational space—a raised wooden deck—was added.*

modest expansion of the building—not expansion to the point of filling the building pad. This simple and effective tool can be used in existing neighborhoods where homes are all built to the setback line and have similar ground coverage as long as the height issue can be effectively addressed. In one-story neighborhoods, a new room would be added to the ground floor; this may mean a less drastic cutback in the building pad and a reduction of height to maintain the one-story character of the neighborhood. If remodels in the neighborhood were conversions to Cape Cod style, a tighter setback range would be used. For example, the zoning might have setbacks that permitted a 7,700-square-foot house on a 10,000-square-foot lot while the neighborhood has homes of 1,100 to 1,500 square feet. Revising the setbacks to permit a 3,200-square-foot house would be less damaging.

Building Coverage

Building coverage follows the model of setbacks. Since both regulate only the ground coverage, there are no essential differences between them as a useful technique for regulating teardowns. Building coverage, like setbacks, requires a height standard. The choice between setbacks and building coverage might be the standard currently in use.

Floor Area Ratios (FAR)

The model here is similar but requires a bit more care since floor area is a more precise measure and directly involves the potential of multiple floors. The need to consider height is even more critical because FAR does not distinguish between ground-floor and upper-floor expansion. Using FAR may be a better choice as a tool for regulating teardowns in neighborhoods where there is a mix of housing: ranches, Cape Cods, and two-story units, each built by a different builder, but all having a similar range of sizes.

Height

Height is very important. Both the number of stories and roof pitches are likely to be common features of the neighborhood. Dramatic changes in height can be a problem. In ranch, Cape Cod, or split-level neighborhoods, it is very likely the maximum height established by zoning district regulations is substantially higher than current building heights. Thus, those standards should be rolled back to a level that respects the existing character. Even in two-story areas, the original homes may have low roof pitches— 5/12, for example. With end gables, adding 15 feet to the rear of a 24-foot-wide house would raise the roof from five feet to a little more than eight feet. If the remodeling involved a change in roof pitch to 9/12, the roof height would nearly triple, from five feet to more than 14.6 feet. The three-foot change would be noticeable, but not threatening, while a 9.6-foot change is similar to an added story and would alter the character.

Building Volume Ratio (BVR)

Building volume Ratio (BVR) remains the most flexible of the regulations because any change is automatically tracked and forces the architect to make trade-offs. In general, use of BVR as the primary regulatory tool in dealing with teardowns is not recommended in existing neighborhoods because it requires so much explanation and a change in the regulation format with which residents are familiar. (Also see page 51 above.)

There is one exception to this—a community or neighborhood where there is a significant gradient in size reflecting historic development patterns. In many New England seaport towns, for example, there may be a shift from captain's houses to small historic Cape Cods within blocks of each other. While it is possible to attempt to break the neighborhood into

Building volume Ratio (BVR) remains the most flexible of the regulations because any change is automatically tracked and forces the architect to make trade-offs.

smaller units with an overlay to designate areas of different BVRs, this may result in mapping battles with some homeowners wanting to move the boundary lines of overlay districts for their own advantage. Thus, the building volume can be tied to a radius around the lot in question so that lines for overlay districts do not need to be drawn.

ADDITIONAL MEASURES

The five controls above are all that is really needed if action is taken early enough. They should be able to accommodate the types of actions residents are currently taking to upgrade their homes.

There are several additional strategies that may be useful if regulations are being formulated in a neighborhood where the teardown process has already begun. Because there are likely to be different views within the neighborhood, more flexibility to increase house size would produce less opposition to the regulations. Community character is not completely related to house size in mature neighborhoods because trees have also matured. The little 1.5-inch tree that was seven to eight feet high when the subdivision was developed is now 40 to 60 feet high. Vegetation is equally important in determining the character of the neighborhood. A very strict requirement to preserve front yard vegetation will be helpful. Two additional volume measures enable an increase in floor area or BVR to be offset by increases in landscape volume ratio.

Landscape Volume Ratio (LVR)

Landscape Volume Ratio (LVR) is a parallel to the BVR but measures the soft vegetative volume, which, in mature residential communities, is as important as building volume since the streets are likely to be lined with mature trees and the landscaping on the lot is likely to be mature as well. In many older neighborhoods, in fact, the landscape volume may be larger than the building volume. The construction of a too-big teardown is likely to result in a loss of mature vegetation, further exacerbating the loss of character as a result of the teardown. The LVR provides a means of measuring this element of the neighborhood character. (Also see page 52 above.)

Site Volume Ratio (SVR)

Site Volume Ratio (SVR) combines the two volume measures, BVR and LVR, and is calculated by subtracting the BVR from the LVR. Thus, a positive SVR indicates a landscape volume greater than the building volume, and a negative value indicates building volume is the dominant value. The SVR is a means of calculating the existing community character in a manner accounting for both the building and the landscaping.

The SVR introduces some flexibility in that it rewards the landowner who preserves existing trees and plants new trees with more volume. The landowner who seeks to cut down existing trees to make room for expansion would have a reduced building volume. Once the teardown process has begun, every bit of flexibility in the regulations will be valuable to the proponents of teardowns, and, if community character is retained, those seeking to eliminate or limit the teardowns are less likely to adamantly oppose teardowns.

The precision and flexibility of the SVR makes it easier to demonstrate the impact of options. For example, a family may have fallen in love with a house plan with 10-foot ceilings and a 9/12 roof pitch, but the house is over the SVR. The relative impact of different ceiling heights or roof pitches can be instantly calculated, so trade-offs between roof, ceilings, and floor areas can be understood. Perhaps only one room needs the higher ceiling, and the roof pitch can be retained to meet the regulations. And adding four, 12-foot-high evergreen trees might avoid resizing one room.

The Site Volume Ratio (SVR) introduces some flexibility in that it rewards the landowner who preserves existing trees and plants new trees with more volume. The landowner who seeks to cut down existing trees to make room for expansion would have a reduced building volume.

CHAPTER 6

Code Language

A number of communities have been struggling with the problems of monotony, Monopoly-set houses, too-big houses, and teardowns for years. In this chapter, we explore a number of solutions from different ordinances around the nation.

The first key to drafting effective regulations is to ensure that the problem is widely recognized as a problem and that the regulations truly *focus* on one or more of the four problems identified in this PAS Report. The issues will be of differing importance to communities. In seeking to deal with any of these issues, citizens and builders may well take exception to any government attempt to deal with aesthetics through regulation. There remain many who will argue that aesthetics is not an area where local government should be involved or have regulations despite the fact that the U.S. Supreme Court has upheld regulations governing aesthetics (see, for example, PAS Report No. 489/490, *Aesthetics and Land-Use Controls,* and importantly for issues of administration, PAS Report No. 454, *Design Review*).

The monotony and Monopoly-set house regulations will certainly be considered by many to be aesthetic regulation. In presenting strategies and regulatory language, one approach is to avoid the architectural *regulation* issue and, instead, to focus on simple regulations that camouflage monotony or the Monopoly-set house. Thus, the discussion of model codes begins with landscaping regulations—greenery hides a multitude of sins. Strong landscaping and tree preservation regulations can be very effective at camouflaging the visual effects of the too-big house and the out-of-scale teardown, in particular.

The second type of regulations is not really aesthetic regulation at all; rather, they are zoning or subdivision techniques with aesthetic implications. The zoning strategies, like the landscaping strategies, all have multiple purposes beyond pure aesthetics. If done well, they may be enough to curb the worst problems.

The following sections provide combined regulations to address Monopoly-set housing and monotony problems. We recommend these be combined because the regulations dealing with one problem offer benefits for the other. The too-big house bulk regulations will follow. Lastly, we will discuss teardown regulations.

REGULATIONS ADDRESSING THE PROBLEMS OF MONOTONY AND MONOPOLY-SET HOUSING
Landscaping Strategies

Landscaping can combat monotony through camouflage. If you see less of the building, it is more difficult to determine if two units are the same. Other PAS Reports also discuss tree conservation ordinances and landscaping standards. Those include PAS Reports Nos. 431, 445, and 489/490.

Street trees. Simple attention to civic beauty can go a long way or have a large impact with relatively minor costs to the home builders. Street tree ordinances can have a dramatic long-term impact. Requirements of two or three street trees per 100 feet of street frontage are the norm for good long-term impact. Many communities do not require the planting of street trees, and, in others, the standard is inadequate. One tree per lot is a badly flawed landscaping standard. Such a standard fails to address corner lots and, on any lots exceeding 50 feet of frontage, the level of planting is inadequate. Lots of one to five acres have used the street-tree approach to create hedgerows that create an almost rural feel as the trees mature.

A far more intensive approach may be appropriate in estate-type developments with lots of an acre or more. Long Grove, Illinois, has a street tree ordinance that basically requires a hedgerow to be planted. The hedgerow approach screens for monotony, Monopoly-set houses, and the too-big house.

*In presenting strategies and regulatory language, one approach is to avoid the architectural **regulation** issue and, instead, to focus on simple regulations that camouflage monotony or the Monopoly-set house.*

LONG GROVE, ILLINOIS, ZONING ORDINANCE

Section 6-5-5 E, October 2001

(E) Street Trees: Street trees shall be planted on each side of the road. The planting requirement is as follows:

  1. The following vegetation shall be planted on each side of the road for each one hundred (100) lineal feet.

      (a) Three three-inch native hardwood canopy trees.

      (b) Three two-inch native hardwood canopy trees.

      (c) Two 1.5-inch understory/ornamental trees.

      (d) Fifteen three-foot shrubs.

  2. The plants shall be grouped or clustered in accordance with the final landscape plan. The final landscape plan shall ensure that corners and areas where a perpendicular street would result in automobile lights shining into the property are densely planted. The plant materials shall screen any such house from vehicular lights.

  3. The plants shall be of species on the approved Long Grove landscape list and shall conform to the specifications in the final landscape plan.

  4. All dead, diseased, or nonthriving landscape vegetation shall be replaced in a timely fashion by the developer for the first two growing seasons occurring after the date of acceptance of the landscape installation by the village. The developer shall provide a maintenance contract to cover the two (2) year period to ensure adequate watering and care. After that time period, the landscape vegetation shall be maintained in good health by the property owner. All such trees shall be considered as protected trees pursuant to section 5-16-6 of this code regardless of size or species and shall be removed and replaced only with the approval of the village in accordance with those provisions.

  5. All roads, utilities, and street landscaping shall be located in an outlot or road right of way. If the road is a private road, the covenants shall determine who shall maintain the plant material.

  6. The ditch shall be at least 10 feet from the edge of pavement unless specifically coordinated and approved in the landscape and engineering drawings. The following illustration indicates the placement of street, utilities, ditch, and landscaping. Two-thirds of the landscaping shall be located between the ditch and street. Shrubs may be clustered near utility boxes.

One element of landscaping regulation needs particular attention—the time frame. Landscaping needs time to take effect. Houses appear at full mass from the day the roof goes on, but immature trees take years to mature. It takes decades before trees reach their maximum heights, and this causes a major problem for landscaping. The home with a few small saplings in the yard looks as if it is inadequately landscaped. This is even more evident to the local planning commission that reviewed landscape plans showing the trees at mature canopy size or, at a minimum, 20 years into the future.

To address this concern, some communities require home builders to show trees at their planted size as well as normal rendering sizes since trees need approximately 10 years to mature. Figure 6-1 shows street trees newly planted in a New Urbanist development in the early spring—they are nearly invisible. This can be compared to a 25-year-old development with very intensive landscaping (Figure 6-2).

The time factor is a variable that differs from area to area and is also sensitive to the level of maintenance and tree type. In the Pacific Northwest, trees grow much faster than in Illinois or Michigan. Since the East Coast is wetter, trees do better there as well. The Southeast has more rainfall and, thus, faster growth rates. Improper care after planting will stunt the trees growth. In many parts of the country, xeriscape—plants that need little water—is critical since native species are adapted to the natural rainfall of the region. Plant selection is always important because native species adapted to the local climate will do best. Consult a landscape architect or a local forestry extension service at a university.

(Left) **Figure 6-1:** *Stick trees in a Traditional Neighborhood Development (TND) community; (right)* **Figure 6-2:** *Mature trees effectively screen development.*

Front-yard landscaping. Requiring front-yard landscaping adds a second layer of camouflage behind the screen of street trees. This is very important, particularly on small lots where architecture has not been given great thought. The smaller the lot, the more effective a given level of landscaping is at softening the impact of the architecture. Many home builders will have standard landscaping packages that provide minimal landscaping.

Open space landscaping. In cluster, planned developments, or traditional neighborhood developments (TNDs), there will be common open space, and it should be landscaped to minimum standards.

Parking lot landscaping. Parking lots are an important element in improving the character of a community. This is particularly important for apartment and town house developments that rely on parking lots or private alleys that serve as both parking lots and vehicular access. This landscaping standard is even more important in nonresidential districts. See PAS Report 411, *The Aesthetics of Parking*, for more information.

Plant units. Natural landscapes are composed of three layers: canopy trees, understory trees, and shrubs. It is useful to separate conifers from deciduous trees and in some areas adding palm trees to the mix of material. Most landscape regulations concentrate only on the canopy trees. It is beneficial to have landscapes with all three layers, as is provided for in ordinances using performance standards. The plant unit is used to specify the planting of yards, bufferyards, parking areas, and open space. In some communities, these units are used to determine the appropriate "density" of street trees as well.

The following provisions comprehensively cover landscaping requirements for lots, open space, parking lots, and street trees; all use the plant unit as the criterion to apply the standards.

NEW CASTLE COUNTY, DELAWARE, LAND DEVELOPMENT CODE

Article 23, Division 23.100-23.151, adopted December 31, 1997

Division 23.100. Plant Units And Materials
This Division establishes a standard landscaping element called a "plant unit." The plant unit serves as a basic measure of plant material required for all landscaping, except natural areas, or mitigation. The plant unit provides a balance of vegetation.

Section 23.110. Standard Plant Units
Each plant unit alternative in Table 23.110 is generally interchangeable with the standard plant unit. The developer is free to use any one or a combination of alternatives. However, some alternatives are preferred given certain objectives. For example, Alternative Unit D is best suited for the interior of parking lots or other places where clear, low-level views are desired or fences

TABLE 23.110. PLANT UNIT ALTERNATIVES

Plant Unit Alternative	Quantity, Size & Type of Plants Required	Illustration
STANDARD PLANT UNIT	1 3" caliper Canopy Tree 2 1-1/2" caliper Understory 13 3' high Shrubs	
ALTERNATIVE UNIT A*	1 3" caliper Canopy Tree 1 1-1/2" caliper Understory 1 6' high Evergreen Tree 11 3' high Shrubs	
ALTERNATIVE UNIT B*	2 1-1/2" caliper Understory 3 6' high Evergreen Trees 7 3' high Shrubs	
ALTERNATIVE UNIT C*	4 6' high Evergreen Trees 15 3' high Shrubs	
ALTERNATIVE UNIT D**	2 3" caliper Canopy Tree 3 3' high Shrubs	

* Preferred for year-round screen.
** May be required where visibility is required for safe automobile operation.

exist. Where year-round screening is required, Alternative Unit B or C is preferred. In some cases, this Code may specify a specific plant unit, or an alternative plant unit may be required during subdivision or site plan review.

Section 23.120. On-Lot Landscaping
In general, the on-lot landscaping shall be distributed around the lot, planted close to the buildings, or be in some combination of these planting schemes. However, front yards are particularly important to preserving community character. Certain unit types require additional planting material to be planted between front-load garages and the right-of-way or as indicated in Section 23.121.

Section 23.121. Special Residential Landscaping
All residential lots of 12,000 square feet or less or any unit using side-load garages shall install special landscaping in addition to the landscaping required by Table 04.111.

A. **Village House.** Village house street yards shall be landscaped with two additional items. Select two from the following categories. These additions shall be included in one of two ways. The plan shall identify the techniques on each lot or options can be included in the house price and selected by the home purchaser.

1. **Street Property-line Border.**

   a. Stone wall, wood or wrought-iron fence at least three feet in height; or

   b. Hedge with shrubs planted at a maximum of three feet on center; or

   c. A grade change of at least two feet, raising the street yard above the sidewalk grade.

   This option is available only where the natural topography slopes up from the sidewalk on that side of the street. This option must run across at least three consecutive lots and be identified on grading plans to ensure adequate drainage.

2. **Additional Landscaping.**

   a. Two flowering understory trees at 1.5-inch caliper.

   b. Two evergreen trees at least five feet high.

   c. Thirteen decorative evergreen trees in at least five gallon pots.

   d. A perennial flower bed having a minimum of five species over 80 square feet and one understory or evergreen of the size indicated in a and b above.

3. **Structure.** One of the following and 10 flowering or evergreen shrubs at least 24 inches high. These options are not available where a front-load garage is used on a lot with less than 90 feet of frontage.

   a. A roofed porch not enclosed or screened, running three-quarters the width of the house front, and having a minimum width of seven feet.

   b. A masonry or stone patio raised a minimum of 18 inches above the front yard, minimum eight-foot width, and at least 500 square feet.

B. **Lot Line Houses.** Lot line houses shall install an additional 1.5 plant units in the front yard whose purpose, location, and design is to screen the view into the side yard and enhance the privacy of this space. The developer may use hedges or substitute a fence for 80 percent of the shrubs.

C. **Other Single Family Lots less than 12,000 square feet.** These lots shall require an additional plant unit.

D. **Side-Loading Garages.** Where a side-loading garage is permitted in front of the house proper, an extra plant unit shall be required between the street and the side of the garage facing the street, or the developer may propose planting options that in the department's opinion are approximately equal in cost and effectiveness.

E. **Attached and Multifamily.** All attached units shall have on-lot landscaping of one plant unit. The landscaping material shall be distributed in the front, rear, or side yards. In multifamily developments, the yard areas associated with each unit shall be landscaped with five plant units per acre.

Section 23.130. Parking Lot Landscaping

Parking lot landscaping shall be one plant unit per number of parking spaces. . . . Each plant unit shall be planted in a planting island(s) or space with a

FIGURE 23.130: EXAMPLES OF PARKING LOT LANDSCAPING CONFIGURATIONS

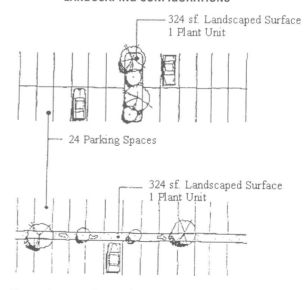

Illustrating: 1.0 Plant Unit per 24 parking spaces

minimum total area of 324 square feet. The plant unit may be distributed between two landscaping islands or in larger continuous islands. If two smaller islands are selected, each shall contain a minimum of 162 square feet in area. In small parking lots, the island(s) may be the lot's corners. The landscaping required…shall be located within the parking lot or adjoining entrance drives and circulation drives. Existing trees that can be preserved by leaving the area under their canopy undisturbed shall count towards the landscaping requirements. Figure 23.130 illustrates appropriate planting areas, preservation of existing trees, and several configurations of one plant unit per 24 parking spaces.

Section 23.140. Standards For Bufferyard Plantings

Table 23.140 depicts the narrowest permitted bufferyard at the top of each opacity category. This is the minimum width of buffer permitted and, if a wall is shown, that is the maximum height permitted. The second standard is wider and may also be used to satisfy the opacity requirement.

FIGURE 23.140. BUFFERYARD OPTIONS FOR A 0.50 OPACITY

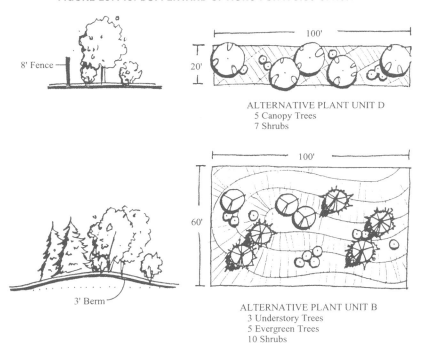

8' Fence

100'

20'

ALTERNATIVE PLANT UNIT D
5 Canopy Trees
7 Shrubs

100'

60'

3' Berm

ALTERNATIVE PLANT UNIT B
3 Understory Trees
5 Evergreen Trees
10 Shrubs

Both provide the widths of bufferyards, the plant materials in plant units, and structures necessary to reach given levels of opacity or buffer type required…. While this table presents only two combinations of bufferyard (width and number of plant units), in actuality, a wide range of other combinations would also meet the respective opacity rating. Flexibility is encouraged; by using the interactive bufferyard system in Section 23.141, the designer may create and test a buffer. The standards are for 100 linear feet of buffer measured at the bufferyard's centerline. Figure 23.140 shows the two bufferyard options set forth to achieve a 0.50 opacity using Section 23.141. Some limited or conditional uses have requirements…that increase bufferyards; these requirements shall be met by adding the opacities of the district bufferyard and the limited or conditional use. For example, if the district requires a 0.3 bufferyard and the specific use requires a 0.2 bufferyard, then a 0.5 bufferyard shall be selected.

Section 23.141 Bufferyards

A. The standards in Table 23.140 have been tested to ensure they meet the opacity standard. Numerous other mixes can meet the standard. The bufferyards were created using the Bufferyard Model. This model is available within the Computerized Land Development Code. Any bufferyard that meets the required opacity rating within

TABLE 23-140. BUFFERYARD REQUIREMENTS PER 100 LINEAR FEET

Opacity	Bufferyad Width (ft.)	Number of Plant Units	Type of Structure Required
"A" Agricultural	200		agricultural land
	20	1	plus 50 thorny bushes
Parking Buffer 1.0	10	0.70	masonry wall or evergreen hedge at 4' oc., or hedge at 3' oc.
	15	1.3	
.10	10	0.85	
	20	0.65	
.20	15	1.55	
	25	1.30	
.30	15	1.80	2 ft. berm
	25	2.10	
.40	20	2.45	4 ft. masonry wall
	30	2.70	
.50	20	2.05	8 ft. fence - 100% opaque
	60	1.40	3 ft. berm
.60	25	2.90	8 ft. fence - 100% opaque
	60	2.65	
.70	30	3.75	8 ft. fence - 100% opaque
	50	4.00	
.80	40	4.10	8 ft. fence - 100% opaque
	80	2.90	
.90	50	4.30	8 ft. masonry wall
	100	2.60	
1.00	50	3.90	8 ft. berm
	100	2.55	3 ft. berm

See Section 23.141 for developing intermediate buffers.

the width limits in Table 23.140 is permitted. The Bufferyard Model can also be used. Table 23.141 lists the settings that shall be used in running the model. This model determines whether or not the tested bufferyard is adequate. The plant type settings are shown but are not to be altered. Only the width of the minimum buffer and height of the structure may be changed. The minimum width is a policy and requires a variance to modify. The height of the structure may be varied only if modifying the parking buffer. Users shall supply the department with a printout of the model run for a buffer that is proposed which shall be verified by the department.

B. Buffers greater than 50 feet wide must meet the height-screening requirement of the model without a berm. Narrower buffers shall be permitted without meeting the model's height screening.

TABLE 23-141. BUFFERYARD MODEL SETTINGS

Factor	Setting	
Building Height	30 ft.	
Viewpoint	140 ft.	
Opacity of Row	0.65	
Minimum Buffer Width	10 ft.	
Plant Unit Area	1,600 sq. ft.	
Plant Unit Unit Compaction	0.50	

Plant Type Settings:

Factor	Canopy	Understory	Conifer	Shrub
Shape	2	3	4	6
Height	26.0	16.0	18.0	3.5
% Opacity	0.85	0.85	1.00	0.80
Standard Plant Unit = a minimum of 507.6 square feet Total Area				
Number	1	2	0	13

Building Height shall be reduced to 5 feet to test parking buffers.

Section 23.150. Street Right-Of-Way
All unpaved areas within street rights-of-way shall be seeded or sodded. Before the release of the 12-month maintenance bond, all unpaved areas between the edge of the road pavement and the right-of-way line shall have:

A. A minimum depth of four inches of topsoil; and,

B. A growth of an acceptable healthy grass turf; and,

C. Trees growing in vigorous, healthy condition and as required in Section 23.151 below.

Section 23.151. Street Trees

A. In new subdivisions or when the development of property occurs, the department shall review, for approval, proposed landscaping plans, and shall require street trees to be planted in any of the parkways and other public places abuttir.g lands henceforth developed and/or subdivided as required in Article 31.

B. Trees shall be planted on each side of the parkway at the minimum rate of one tree per 40 feet of right-of-way. Where lot frontages are less than 40 feet wide along the right-of -way, trees shall be planted at the minimum rate of one tree per lot; on corner lots, a minimum of two trees per lot. Except that on interior streets in nonresidential subdivisions not designated as arterials or collectors, trees shall be planted on each side of the right-of-way at the minimum rate of one tree per 50 feet of right-of-way.

C. Center boulevards shall have a minimum width of 16 feet and shall have one additional tree planted every 40 feet in the landscaped island. Boulevards having a width greater than 20 feet shall plant 1.5 trees every 40 feet.

D. No one right-of-way tree species may make up more than 20 percent of the planting stock of the entire development.

E. *Tree Quality and Size:* All trees planted within rights-of-way shall be balled and burlapped, single-stemmed trunks, branched no lower than six feet above ground and grown in nurseries from the Delaware, Maryland, New Jersey, and Pennsylvania regions. No tree selected for planting shall be less than three inches in diameter as measured six inches above the established ground level. All plants and planting methods shall be in accordance with the American Nurseryman's Association standards.

Averaging lot can have a significant impact on aesthetics because it helps prevent cookie-cutter development.

F. *Minimum Spacing:* No trees may be planted closer together than 30 feet except that special plantings may be clustered as determined appropriate by the Department.

Zoning Strategies

Averaged lots. Averaging lots was a zoning technique that was not initially designed for its aesthetic effects. Its goal was to provide greater flexibility in lot layout and to provide greater diversity in housing products in order to achieve housing goals. The technique does, however, have a significant impact on aesthetics because it helps prevent cookie-cutter development. Figure 6-3, from *Performance Zoning*, illustrates the standard subdivision approach dictated by Euclidian zoning, which results in cookie-cutter design. This type of planning maximizes the monotony issue. In order to ensure predictability, the regulations are based on a standard lot size in the communities. Current zoning also seeks strategies that avoid aesthetic regulations. Table 6-1 illustrates the nature of these regulations. Note that this strategy is also used in attached single-family homes.

Source: Kendig 1980, 20

Figure 6-3. The standard subdivision approach to laying out lots, which results in cookie-cutter development

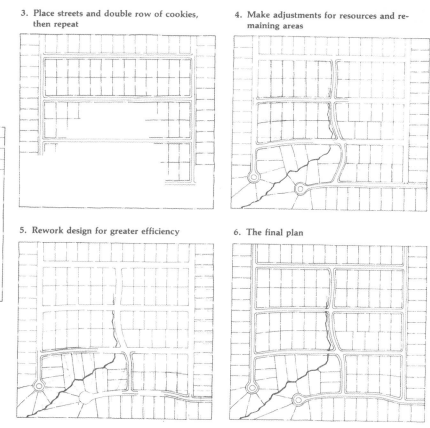

TABLE 6-1. LOT AND BUILDING STANDARDS

| District | Minimum | | | | | | Maximum |
	Lot Area (square feet)	Lot Width (feet)	Street Yard (feet)	Side Yard (feet)	Rear Yard (feet)	Unit Mix (percent)	Building Height (feet)
Suburban Transition	5,500	50	25	6	20	20	32
	6,600	60	25	6	20	40	32
	7,700	70	25	6	20	15	32
Traditional Neighborhood	4,800	48	12 build to	5	25	20	32
	5,400	54	12 build to	5	25	40	32
	6,000	60	12 build to	5	25	15	32

Note that the three lot sizes—small (5,500 square feet), average (6,600 square feet), and large (7,700 square feet)—are module-based on the lot width and depth of the average lot (the depth of all Traditional Neighborhood lots is 100 feet; and 110 feet for Suburban Transition). For this reason, the lot width is placed before the area because it is the control factor. Incidentally, the width difference is more important than the area difference in altering the facade. The code needs to have the following language if it is to be effective in meeting monotony goals:

> The developer shall have different models for each of the three defined lot sizes so that the widths of buildings for each of the three lot widths are proportionate to the difference in lot widths.

This language ensures that models are truly different. Two key elements of the regulations need explanation. First, there is a minimum percentage of three lot sizes in the development, but they do not total to 100 percent in the example. In many other codes that use this approach, the small and medium lots are set at minimums of 25 and 50 percent, respectively, while the remainder are made up of the large lots. This was done to account for rounding to whole numbers of units since subdivisions do not come in 100-unit increments (25 percent may well be 26.3 percent). The percentages can be changed, but the large lot should always be the remainder to keep average lot size accurate from a density perspective. Consider that, if there is a higher percentage of large lots, this could affect density, which is calculated on the average. Conversely, if there is a larger percentage of small lots, there is greater flexibility because they use less land. Creating adequate density this way can be part of an affordable housing strategy. It should be noted that this is not a problem in performance ordinances where the density is calculated on the average size; in such ordinances, the use of more large lots would reduce density below the maximum.

Alley access. Alley access is an important strategy for traditional community design. It is included here because the smaller the lot, the greater the impact of the garage. As the width of the house declines, garages take up more and more of the total lot width. There is almost nothing that can be done to distinguish homes when garages are dominant, so forcing the units to have alley access allows architecture a chance to break up monotony.

With townhouses, the garage takes up nearly all the lot. Typically, the land development regulations would require alleys on every block. This can create problems where one side of the street faces open space. The code

Alley access is an important strategy for traditional community design.

should contain specific language permitting alleys to be deleted where the units abut open space:

> All units shall have both a street and alley frontage, except where the lots back to open space. No alleys shall be permitted where lots back to open space, and periodic breaks shall be provided that provide pedestrian access to open space. Such areas shall be landscaped with at least two trees and 10 shrubs to provide a visual break in the streetscape.

Building pads. Building pad regulations have been applied in planned unit developments (PUDs) and are not a requirement in any ordinance we have seen. Such a requirement applies only in large-lot situations— lots greater than one acre with minimum frontage of at least 120 feet. At this size, the average building does not maximize the area between side-yard setbacks. The building pad approach is also valuable when there are natural resources that can be better preserved if the building's location can be adjusted on the lot. The code language might prescribe the following:

> Home builders may be required to use building pads, rather than setback lines, to provide greater interest in design, preserve trees or other resources, take advantage of soil conditions, or make the development more suburban in character. Building pads would be moved to provide irregular spacing of buildings and to break up the linearity of the street facade of buildings. The building pads shall be recorded on the final plat in lieu of setback lines.

The building pad approach permits houses to be set at angles on the lot and for the front setbacks to be varied significantly. These variations use perspective or viewing angles to alter the appearance of a unit. This adds a whole new dimension to the view of the unit and allows landscape to alter a unit's appearance with respect to its neighbors, as opposed to having the units lined up parallel to the street with a uniform setback.

MONOPOLY-SET REGULATIONS

The regulations governing Monopoly-set housing are intended to create better design to make homes more attractive. They seek to address the blandness of production housing by making roofs provide visual interest and eliminating the fancy false front and drab side and rear styles.

Roof Overhangs

Require a roof overhang on all residential units. The larger the overhang, the more pronounced the shadow line. The following code language is taken from the Lake Villa, Illinois, ordinance:

> An important element of design is the shadow lines that are created by roofs and help articulate the building. All homes having pitched roofs shall have eaves that extend a sufficient distance to create shadow lines. A variety of overhangs is desired. The following standards shall apply:
>
> 1. Variety: The subdivision or planned unit development as a whole shall have a variety of different roof overhang profiles.
>
> 2. Extension: The overhang, not including gutters, shall extend at least eight inches beyond the plane of the wall.
>
> 3. Exception: The minimum overhang shall not apply for individual homes built in an historical style where overhangs were not part of the style (Cape Cod, for example) or in a unique individual design. The architectural board shall review the architectural plans for such buildings.

Note the language recognizes there are styles where no overhangs are found. The certification of the architectural review board or some other review body is needed to ensure that the developer does not claim a neo-nothing design is a Cape Cod-style unit.

360-Degree Architecture

The second regulation attempting to address the Monopoly-set house is the 360-degree requirement for building treatment. The minimum standard is that window and door details, trim, and shutters, if used, be used on all elevations of the house. Consider the following language:

> **Window, Door, And Trim**
> The home shall have similar style and quality window, door, trim, and decorative moldings on all exterior building elevations of the home.

Because masonry adds substantially to the cost of a house, the first standard does not mandate uniform materials. The following regulations address materials, as well. As was discussed above, home builders have to be shown how to use this standard to control cost. The requirement that housing be all masonry, in the author's opinion, is an exclusionary tool that increases the cost of housing and can therefore be exclusionary.

> **Building Material**
> Identical or substantially similar siding materials or veneers shall be used on all exterior sides of the home. This does not prohibit the use of veneers or changes of materials on a facade where, for example, materials might change at the second floor or at a windowsill height. Where a wing or projection of the building is offset, the wing or projection may use different materials to give it emphasis, provided the materials are applied to the entire wing or projection.

Note the language limits the use of a single-wall application of masonry by mandating returns and, specifically, provides for the application to a wing or projecting portion of the house.

Blank Walls

Blank walls are another curse of the Monopoly-set house. This is not a problem limited to entry-level housing. It shows up in semi-custom and luxury production units (Figure 6-4). When large homes are close to-

Blank walls are another curse of the Monopoly-set house. This is not a problem limited to entry-level housing. It shows up in semi-custom and luxury production units.

(Above) **Figure 6-4:** *The blank wall: a curse of the Monopoly-set house;* (left) **Figure 6-5:** *False windows on a lot line where privacy is an issue; such an approach is preferable to a blank wall.*

gether, windows are often cut out either because they add cost or the designer has lost sight of the relationship between windows and light. If the architecture cannot eliminate the blank wall or has only a trivial window, the false window is a good answer, as can be seen in Figure 6-5 (a lot-line house where the side yard was all on the other lot, and because it was designed as useable space, the builder limited side windows on the zero lot line side). The false window is relatively inexpensive, provides the needed privacy, and relieves the Monopoly-set appearance of the blank wall.

ANTI-MONOTONY REGULATIONS

All anti-monotony regulations mandate change to the front facades of a house model when that model is used adjoining lots. Figures 2-12 and 2-18 on pages 20 and 27 illustrate two areas that can be changed easily with dramatic results.

The simplest regulations for monotony is to deal with it through mandatory changes to the elevations of a single house model, which includes roof changes, flipping the house, and rotating the house.

CITY OF PAOLA, KANSAS, LAND DEVELOPMENT CODE, 1997

Article 15, Division 15.300: Monotony Standards
In Paola's traditional neighborhoods, buildings were built in small numbers so blocks developed over an extended period. The result is great diversity in scale, style, and detail. Modern development practices often result in large numbers of mass produced housing that is often monotonous and out of character with the City. This Division controls the building of similar buildings in residential subdivisions.

Section 15.310. Measures
The following measures are used to evaluate developments and prevent monotony. Figure 15.310 illustrates the following points.

A. *Floor Plan.* The floor plan defines the arrangement of the building's form, arrangement of rooms, windows, and doors. Identical floor plans can lead to monotony.

B. *Orientation.* This describes the orientation of building floor plan(s). A building rotated 90 degrees will not appear identical even when the floor plans are identical. Similarly, flipping or reversing the floor plan creates a different look.

C. *Rooflines.* Rotating the orientation of the roof peak, or otherwise altering the roofline in a significant manner can alter the appearance completely.

D. *Materials.* Brick; stone; natural-stained wood vertical siding; horizontal siding in wood, fiberglass, or metal; stucco or Dri-vit; and shingles are all considered different exterior materials.

E. *Architectural Features.* The addition of a front porch, tower, or balcony are architectural features that change the facade sufficiently to create a difference.

F. *Color.* Color can be used to provide a unifying sense to a development; it can create monotony; or it can create conflicts.

Section 15.320. Standards
The following standards shall be applied to all single-family dwellings or buildings containing more than one dwelling unit to prevent monotony:

A. A variety of building sizes or scales shall be provided. No more than three buildings in a row shall have less than a 30 percent difference in scale between the largest and smallest building as measured by building floor area. (See Figure 15.320.)

B. No two dwellings or buildings on a street face shall be identical in floor plan or color unless differing by at least two of the following (See Figure 15.310.):

FIGURE 15.310. MEASURES TO GUARD AGAINST MONOTONY

A. FLOOR PLAN

Building Outline

Acceptable   Unacceptable

B. ORIENTATION

Flipped
Rotated

Acceptable   Unacceptable

C. ROOF LINES

Rotated Peak

D. MATERIALS

Materials Variation

E. ARCHITECTURAL FEATURES

Architectural Feature Variation

F. COLOR

Portion of Typical Block

No two buildings shall share identical
color schemes within the same block

1. Rotated or reversed lot orientation.

2. Different roof configuration or orientation.

3. Different materials or exterior walls. A mix of materials may be used on buildings. For example, stone and shingle or brick and horizontal siding.

4. The addition of architectural features that alter the appearance.

5. Identical color schemes shall require the addition of another differentiating feature (total of 3) from numbers 1 through 4 above to offset the similarity in color.

C. Buildings having more than one unit shall include different floor plans, staggered alignments with the street, roofline variation, architectural features, or rotated orientation to achieve interest in the building.

D. Design Review. In some cases, as with attached units or subdivisions that seek to replicate a historic theme or themes, greater unity of design may actually enhance the character of the area. Such plans shall be permitted only where the developer submits architectural, landscaping, and sign reviews, and receives planning commission approval.

FIGURE 15.320. SIZE AND SCALE VARIATIONS

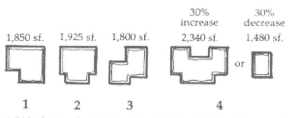

			30% increase	30% decrease
1,850 sf.	1,925 sf.	1,800 sf.	2,340 sf.	1,480 sf.
1	2	3	4	

1,800 sf. (smallest lot) x 1.3 = 2,340 sf. (30% difference)
1,925 sf. (largest lot)/1.3 = 1,480 sf. (30% difference)

Communities go through a learning curve on monotony control. This chapter began with the first Long Grove code. The village was lucky with the first small-lot cluster development because the developer was very concerned with not having similarity between adjoining units.

The second small-lot development was a PUD, and the village knew it would be dealing with a production home builder. The village attempted to provide a monotony code for this PUD. The builder was required to provide guidelines for the differentiation between facades of different models. The developer chose to use architectural styles as the means of differentiation. The original developer intended to sell to a builder and, thus, did not have models to approve.

The village required the developer to provide guidelines for components of each style. Drawings were submitted and approved, but the developer was not required to use all the elements of the style. Styles included Tudor, prairie, craftsman, nineteenth-century farm, and Victorian. Unfortunately, the building official was not up to the task of enforcing strict conformance with the historical precedents of each style. As a result, even though Tudor and prairie historically used casement windows rather than double-hung windows, all the units share the same double-hung windows and all use the same standard widths. The Tudor, as well, would typically have had narrower windows than most of the other styles. Figure 6-6 shows four of the houses.

Figure 6-6: The four styles of houses in a Long Grove, Illinois, subdivision as a response to the village's anti-monotony code (clockwise from upper left: craftsman, prairie, Victorian, Tudor).

There are several ways of administering monotony codes. The best method is to require the developer to get approval for all housing models and elevation options. This enables the community to do an initial check, using planning staff or a design review committee. Figure 6-7 illustrates the sheet of model examples that would be presented to a community who had an anti-monotony process in place. These sheets should be annotated to highlight differences and educate the reviewers. This method is superior to the house-by-house approval method since the building officer may have limited training and insufficient time to do a thorough review on a case-by-case basis. Figures 6-8, 6-9, and 6-10 show some of the actual houses approved.

The code from Lake Villa, Illinois, provides a detailed method for evaluating models that are intended to have a uniform character but still provide interest and variety.

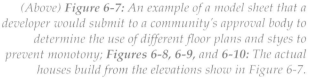

(Above) **Figure 6-7:** *An example of a model sheet that a developer would submit to a community's approval body to determine the use of different floor plans and styes to prevent monotony;* **Figures 6-8, 6-9,** *and* **6-10:** *The actual houses build from the elevations show in Figure 6-7.*

VILLAGE OF LAKE VILLA, ILLINOIS, ZONING ORDINANCE

Article 8

Section I. Residential Design Standards

A. Purpose: The residential design standards of this section are intended to ensure that residential subdivisions in the Village are varied and interesting in character and that they provide a range of housing choices.

B. Applicability: All residential subdivisions and residential developments containing more than 20 lots or 20 dwelling units shall be subject to the standards of this section.

C. Lot Width and Unit Type Variety: The developer/builder shall provide a sufficient number of floor plans and building elevation options (with distinctly different appearance) to allow compliance with the anti-monotony standards of this section.

D. Village Review: All building elevations to be used within the subdivision/development shall be reviewed by the planning commission and village board prior to approval of the final subdivision plat or site plan. At the time of review, the developer shall also present to the planning commission and village board plans for ensuring on-going compliance with the General Design Standards and Anti-Monotony Standards during build-out of the development. The village board shall have final decision-making authority to approve or deny the proposed elevations and plans for compliance, based on whether such elevations and plans comply with the standards of this section.

E. General Design Standards:

   1. Roof Overhangs: Roofs shall have eaves that extend at least 12 inches beyond the plane of the exterior wall. This standard may be waived only when the building strictly adheres to a historical architectural

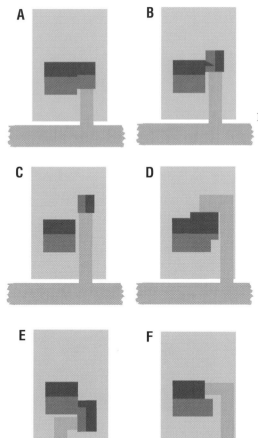

Figure 6-11: *Garage orientation: A. Front-load Garage; B. Front-load setback garage; C. Rear garage; D. Rear-load garage; E. Side-load front garage; F. Side-load garage.*

style that does not include eaves, as confirmed by the latest edition of *A Field Guide to American Houses*.

2. Roof Heights: At least 10 percent of the units within the development shall be ranch or 1.5-story dwellings.

3. Window and Door Trim: Window, door and trim elements shall be similar on all four building elevations. The intent of this provision is to require four-sided architecture.

F. Anti-monotony Standards: Buildings on adjoining lots or on opposing lots shall not have a similar appearance. Therefore, no single model or floor plan using the same elevation package shall be built on the first two lots on either side of the subject house or on the five opposing lots immediately across the street. (See drawing attached as Figure 8.1-F – Adjoining and Opposing Lots.) However, the same model may be built on the four adjoining or five opposing lots if the floor plans of abutting units are flipped and the units are of different color and the proposal complies with one of the following three options:

1) Unique Architectural Style: If all houses within the subdivision have a distinctly recognized architectural style that is generally true to the unique characteristics of that style and historical period, as approved by the Village Planner or Board-designate. Architectural styles shall be evaluated using the most recent edition of *A Field Guide to American Houses*. The style shall use traditional roof pitches, architectural detailing and trim, materials, window details and fenestration, and eave treatment carried out over all elevations; or

2) Masonry: All building elevations are finished in brick or stone; or

3) Design Variations: The houses are different in at least four of the following ways:

a. Garage Orientation: The garage orientation between the units being compared is different (e.g., external side-load corner lot, internal side-load corner, front-load, side-load front, rear-load or detached);

b. Porch: When the units being compared both have front porches, both porches shall have a minimum depth of seven feet and one shall be a one-story and the other shall be a two-story porch;

c. Window Placement and Design: The units being compared have windows that are substantially different in dimension and placement on the front facades, and windows and trim are completely different in design, width, shape, fenestration, and trim and detail color;

d. Combination of Materials: A combination of materials are used on all building elevations, provided that the combination does not consist of aluminum siding combined with vinyl siding;

e. Garage Roofs: Garage roofs are differentiated by hipped framing or by adding gables or dormers:

f. Garage Doors: One of the houses being compared has single-wide garage doors and the other has double-wide garage doors;

Figure 6-12: *(Left) Double-wide garage door; (right) Single-wide garage doors.*

g. Bonus Room: One of the houses being compared has a room that is added so as to alter the front façade elevation by adding an addition (over the garage, a second-story room or ground-floor addition) that provides at least an additional 150 square feet of floor area;

h. Masonry Materials: The building uses masonry (brick or stone) on not less than 50% and not more than 99 percent of the front façade of the building and is wrapped around both sides to an appropriate break line or quoined on the corners;

Figure 6-13: (Left) Base house: (center) Bonus room; (right) Bonus room 2.

   i. Masonry Front Façade: At least one of t he houses being compared has masonry applied to 100 percent of the front façade;

   j. Front-Load Garage Setback of Eight Feet or More: Where a front-load garage incorporates a garage setback of between eight and 15 feet from the house's front façade. Front porches shall be counted as the front wall only where they are at least 84 square feet in area and 12 feet in length.

The following provisions from Georgetown, Texas, use housing type as an indicator of difference (see provisions under "Differentiation"). Another provision uses the number of stories in a building to avoid monotony. If one uses both Differentiation options 1 and 2, there will always be a very different appearance. The first criteria might have been better if it required a different floor plan or model rather than just type. The requirement based on number of stories might have been strengthened by prescribing differences in height, which would introduce differences in both plan and bulk elements, greatly enhancing diversity. The roof rotation provision is a strong tool but not on all roof types. The code does give credit for rotating a hip or mansard roof. Rotation works only if the floor plan is rotated 90 degrees and the building is rectangular not square.

GEORGETOWN, TEXAS, ANTI-MONOTONY PROVISIONS

Requirements for Single-Family Residential Buildings

A. Similarity Restricted

No Building Permit shall be issued for any new single-family dwelling unit, which is similar in appearance to any dwelling unit near the proposed building, as further defined below.

The following dwelling units or projects shall be exempt from the provisions of this Section.

1. Dwellings for which a Building Permit was approved before the effective date of this UDC, including dwellings that are being remodeled, reconstructed or replaced after damage by fire, windstorm or other casualty.

2. Subdivisions already in progress, and developing under the provisions of Section 1.03 (applicability).

3. Houses not within subdivisions.

4. Houses in the Ag, RE or RL Districts.

5. Multifamily projects, including apartments.

6. Planned Unit Developments in which similarity of architectural form and style among dwelling is integral to the success of a unified plan.

Calculation of Differences in Appearance

1. Differences in bulk and massing shall be reviewed for two lots on either side of the proposed unit on the same side of the street.

2. Where lots are interrupted by an intervening street, Parkland, or similar feature of at least 50 feet in width, no review shall be necessary.

3. The proposed unit shall be considered different from any vacant lot for which no Building Permit has been issued without requiring further documentation.

Differentiation

The proposed unit shall differ from each other reviewed house in at least two of the five criteria listed below, unless the units differ with respect to the number of full stories, then only #2 is required.

1. The unit is a different housing type.

    a. Single-family detached;

    b. Zero lot line; or

    c. Single-family attached.

2. The unit differs in the number of full stories.

    a. Single-story; or

    b. Two-story.

3. The unit is served by a different type of garage.

    a. Front-load garage (one-car, two-car, three-car);

    b. Side-load garage;

    c. Detached garage; or

    d. Carport.

4. The unit has a different roof type.

    a. Gable;

    b. Hip;

    c. Gambrel;

    d. Mansard;

    e. Roof types a. through d. rotated 90 degrees; or

    f. Flat.

5. The unit has variation in the articulation of the front façade.

    a. Garage setback from the front façade of at least 4 feet;

    b. Covered, open walled porch of at least 6 feet in depth extending at least 33 percent of the width of the front façade; or

    c. Other articulation of the front façade at least 4 feet in depth, extending at least 33 percent of the width of the front façade.

Permit Review

Acceptable documentation may include photographs of the other structures in question (no building elevations are required)

1. A subdivision or phase thereof may be reviewed as a whole for conformity with this requirement, provided that adequate documentation to ensure conformity is submitted with the plat. Such documentation is not required to be recorded as part of the plat.

2. The Building Official shall review the submitted documentation and any previously-approved Building Permits and make a determination. Where the Building Official finds that a dwelling for which a Building Permit is being requested is similar in appearance based on the standards above, the permit shall be denied.

Anti-monotony provision can also be used to address the problem of the Monopoly-set house. The 360-degree rule and detailing are evident in Figure 6-14 (an early 1950s house with good detailing). Contrasting Figure 6-14 with Figure 6-15 illustrates the power of a changed roof alignment. The houses in Figure 6-14 and 6-15 are the same "boxes," but from different eras; the roof in Figure 6-14 makes this a "gable end" house, whereas the roof of the house in Figure 6-15 makes it a "gable front" house. It is useful to contrast these two simple homes with the much larger, modern home where all the attention is often lavished on the front elevation leaving the side and rear unadorned. It is possible to try too hard, as illustrated in Figure 6-16. The facade is "junked up" with too much activity, and four different materials are pasted together on the side elevation.

(Above, left) **Figure 6-14:** *A 1950s small "gable end" house with good detailing; (above right)* **Figure 6-15:** *The "front gabled" house; (below, left)* **Figure 6-16:** *The modern house, "junked up" with a variety of materials.*

REGULATIONS FOR THE TOO-BIG HOUSE

In this section, we will use the Long Grove, Illinois, provisions again to illustrate a progression, since it has gone to two sets of building bulk regulations and, as of the publication of this PAS Report, is holding hearings on a third. The first set of bulk controls was the use of standard setbacks; the second was the institution of a floor area control measure.

Table 6-2 compares the standard one-, two-, and three-acre lots under the setback regulations and floor area controls. Note that the setbacks were virtually unlimited given the possible one-story building sizes.

TABLE 6-2. COMPARISON OF MAXIMUM FLOOR AREAS UNDER SETBACKS AND BULK REGULATIONS		
	Floor Area within with Setbacks (one story)	Floor Area Under Bulk Regulations
One-acre lot	18,936	8,789
Two-acre lot	36,900	9,889
Three-acre lot	53,280	10,978

Source: Long Grove, Illinois, Zoning Ordinance

The floor area control is not based on a single FAR, but adjusts as lot size changes. This was done because the vast majority of the housing in Long Grove was done as a Planned Unit Development, so, although the three residential districts had minimum lot sizes (one, two, and three acres), the actual developments have lots from 8,000 square feet to five acres. Since lot size actually varies by development, rather than zoning district, a universal bulk formula was needed. Because of the range in lot sizes, a single FAR would not have controlled property at all ends of the range. In most communities, each zoning district would need its own bulk control standard matched to the lot size in the zoning district. In performance zoning ordinances, the housing types and lot sizes within a type are independent of the district. A village or traditional house, for example, would be permitted as a single-family option in all residential districts. Thus, in most performance ordinances, bulk is regulated by housing type.

VILLAGE OF LONG GROVE, ILLINOIS, ZONING ORDINANCE, 1990

Chapter 15

5-15-1: "Floor Area" Defined:
For the purposes of this chapter, the term "floor area" shall mean the sum of the gross floor area for each of a building's stories as measured from the exterior limits of the faces of the structure. For all uses, except single-family detached dwellings, the floor area of a building includes basement floor area. Dormers and attic areas shall count as gross floor area if there is a headroom of 7.5 feet. All attic areas with 7.5 feet of headroom shall be included in the gross floor area. Attached roofed porches shall be included in gross floor area. For single-family detached dwellings, the gross floor area does not include basement floor areas, but gross floor area does include one-half of the entire gross floor area for all walk-out type basements. Floor area shall include the floor area of any attached garage. In rooms where there is a ceiling in excess of 16 feet in height to the highest point of the ceiling, the floor area of these rooms shall be counted twice.

5-15-2: Floor Area Of Principal Building:
Within the R1, R2, or R3 zoning district, the floor area of the principal building on any given lot or parcel shall be in conformity with the standards set forth in section 5-15-3 of this chapter.

5-15-3: Maximum Floor Area Formula:

RANGE	LOT SIZE CALCULATION FOR MAXIMUM FLOOR AREA
10,000 sq. ft. to 43,559 sq. ft	5,500 sq. ft. building size + 0.098 sq. ft. of building area for each sq. ft. of lot area over 10,000 sq. ft. In no case shall a principal building exceed 8,800 sq. ft.
43,560 sq. ft. to 130,679 sq. ft.	8,800 sq. ft. building size + 0.025 sq. ft. of building area for each sq. ft. of lot area over 43,560 sq. ft. In no case shall a principal building exceed 11,000 sq. ft.
130,680 sq. ft. and greater	11,000 sq. ft. building size + 0.022 sq. ft. of building area for each sq. ft. of lot area over 130,680 sq. ft. Where a principal building is 11,000 sq. ft. or greater, for each 1,000 sq. ft. or fraction thereof over 10,000 sq. ft., the front yard setback shall be increased an additional 50 ft. In no case shall a principal building exceed 13,000 sq. ft.

5-15-4: Conflict:
In the event of a conflict between the terms and conditions of this chapter and the maximum lot coverage provisions of subsections 5-4-2-4(D), 5-4-3-4(D), and 5-4-4-4(D) of this title, the more stringent provision shall prevail, so that the standard yielding the smaller principal structure would prevail.

5-15-5: Variance:
No variance shall be granted from the terms of this chapter. The general variance provisions of chapter 12 of this title shall not apply to this chapter.

As lot size increased and the village experienced its first luxury production housing development, the need for a new bulk regulation was evident. The current draft of the new regulations is a building volume regulation along with a recommendation to require front yard landscaping in addition to street trees.

PROPOSED AMENDMENT TO LONG GROVE ZONING, AS OF MAY 2003

Definitions

average ground elevation The average elevation at the foundation of the building, based on the finished grades on all walls of the building. Measurements shall be taken at every change in plane of the exterior wall and at any change in grade slope as a result of grading or retaining walls. Window wells or door wells that provide outside access shall not be included unless they extend further than four feet beyond the foundation. If the Village finds that the number of elevations is designed to reduce the average grade by more than six inches, the zoning officer may add elevation spots on the low wall.

building height The vertical distance from the average ground elevation adjacent to the structure and the highest point of the roof. For flat roof structures, height shall be to the top of parapet walls. Chimneys, spires, towers, elevator penthouses, tanks and similar projections, but not including signs, shall not be included in calculating the height provided no such feature occupies more than 5 percent of the roof area.

Building Volume (BV): The total building volume measured to the outside of the building walls and roof. It includes all area above the final finished grade. It also includes the volume enclosed by porches.

plant unit A grouping of plant material used to specify new landscaping requirements. There are five alternative mixes of plant material that may be used. The following table indicates the mix of plant material:

Table of Alternative Plant Units (1)						
Plant Type	Plant Size	Alternative One (Street Trees)	Alternative Two	Alternative Three	Alternative Four	Alternative Five (Parking Lots or with Fences)
Canopy Tree	3-inch caliper	1	1	0	1	2
Canopy Tree	2-inch caliper	1	0	1	1	0
Understory	1.5- inch caliper	1	2	1	0	1
Evergreen	8 ft.	0	1	3	1	0
Shrubs	3 ft.	8	8	1	6	0

5-15-1: Maximum Building Bulk
Residential dwelling units shall not exceed the maximum building volume (BV) permitted by this section. To determine the BV, use the formulas in the following table, Formulas to Calculate BV, for the lot size range in which the proposed lot area is found.

Formulas Used to Calculate Building Volume	
Lots 6,000 to 9,999 square feet	$BV=((2,120+(LA-6,000))x0.25x14.90196)+7,200$
Lots 10,000 to 43,559 square feet	$BV=((3,120+(LA-10,000))x0.10x14.90196)+10,800$
Lots 43,560 to 130,679 square feet	$BV=((6,480+(LA-43,560))x0.034x15.39216)+10,800$
Lots 130,680 to 435,600 square feet*	$BV=((9,540+(LA-130,680))x0.025x15.88235)+14,400$
LA = Lot Area of Proposed Lot exclusive of road or road access easements.	
*Lots in excess of 435,600 square feet shall have a BVR based on 435,600 square foot lots.	

For example, a 20,000-square-foot lot has a maximum BV of 72,494 cubic feet. Any BV less than or equal to 72,494 cubic feet would be permitted.

5-15-2: Conflict
In the event of a conflict between the terms and conditions of this chapter and the maximum lot coverage, the more stringent provision shall prevail, so that the standard yielding the smaller principal structure would prevail.

5-15-3: Variance
No variance shall be granted from the terms of this Section 5-15-3.

This variance provision is important because there is no rational for a house to be larger than the maximum size. There can be no hardship that requires a landowner to have a larger house than is permitted for everybody else; no unique requirement would create this.

A more radical solution is to switch to a site volume ratio (SVR) that accounts for landscaping, tree preservation, and building volumes. This approach has the advantage that a landowner may seek to mitigate a too-big house by adding landscaping or preserving existing trees.

The disadvantage of this approach is twofold. First, it requires an individual lot analysis that landowners must conduct. Second, building officers fear that landowners will take down trees after receiving occupancy permits, thus creating difficult enforcement issues.

The following draft regulations from Long Grove, Illinois, provide the additional standards needed for a site volume regulation. It includes definitions of landscape volume, and site volume, plus a revised table based on site volume ratios rather than building volume.

DRAFT REGULATIONS FOR LONG GROVE, ILLINOIS

Using Site Volume Ratio

Building Volume (BV): This is the total building volume measured to the outside of the building walls and roof. It includes all area above the final finished grade. It also includes the volume enclosed by porches, decks, or stairs more than four feet above grade.

Building Volume Ratio (BVR): This is calculated by dividing the building volume by 10 and dividing again by the area of the lot (in square feet).

$$BVR = (BV/10)/\text{Lot Area (in square feet)}$$

Landscape Volume (LV): This is the volume of landscape planted or existing on the site. The volume of new plant material should be calculated by using plant units whose volumes shall be considered to be 4,096 cubic feet. The number of plant units rounded to one decimal shall be used to determine the landscape volume by multiplying plant units by 4,096. For existing trees preserved in a conservation easement on the lot, the area under the canopy shall be mapped and multiplied by sixteen (16).

Landscape Volume Ratio (LVR): This is calculated by dividing the landscape volume by ten (10) and dividing again by the area of the lot (in square feet).

$$LVR = (LV/10)/\text{ Lot Area (in square feet)}$$

Plant Unit: The plant unit is a grouping of plant material used to specify new landscaping requirements. There are three alternative mixes of plant material that may be used. The following table indicates the mix of plant material.

Alternative Plant Units (2)				
Plant Type	Plant Size	Alternative 1 (Street Trees)	Alternative 2	Alternative 3
Canopy Tree	3-inch caliper	1	1	0
Canopy Tree	2-inch caliper	1	0	0
Understory	1.5-inch caliper	1	1	2
Evergreen	8 ft.	0	1	2
Shrubs	3 ft.	5	1	8

Site Volume (SVR): This is a combined measure that uses both the building volume and landscape volume. It is calculated by taking the Landscape Volume Ratio and subtracting the Building Volume Ratio.

$$SVR = LVR - BVR$$

5-15-1: MAXIMUM BUILDING BULK

Residential dwelling units shall not exceed the minimum site volume ratio (SVR) permitted by this section. The tables below indicate the maximum SVR that is permitted on lots of various sizes. As long as the SVR of the

SITE VOLUME RATIO CHART

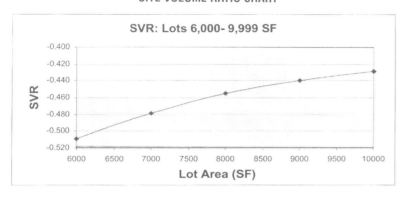

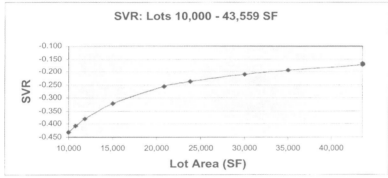

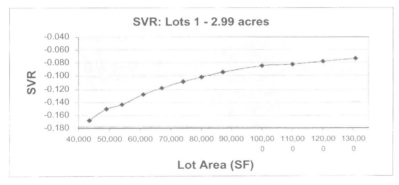

proposed building is higher than that indicated in the tables, the building is in conformance. For example, a 20,000 square foot lot has a minimum SVR of -0.206. Any SVR larger than -0.206, such as -.180, would be permitted.

The Long Grove SVR model shall be used to calculate the exact minimum SVR values for lots, rather than interpolating from the chart. The developer shall provide the building volume, building coverage, lot area (excluding street area from the center line to the back of the ditch where the street is not contained in an outlot or public right-of-way), width of the lot, and number of plant units to be planted. The Village will run the SVR model to determine if the proposed building meets the standard.

The Long Grove SVR model may also be used to evaluate a lot's potential prior to designing a house. The model permits the entry of information on a lot, the house, and landscaping. In this model, the developer may set the height of floors, number of stories, building width, garage bays, bay size and roof pitch to approximate the desired product. In addition, landscaping may be added to mitigate building volume. This permits the developer to control variables that effect the ultimate site volume ratio. A higher roof pitch would result in lower floor area, for example.

5-15-2: CALCULATING LANDSCAPE VOLUME ON SITES WITH EXISTING TREES

When calculating the landscape volume on sites with existing trees or wooded sites, the area to be included in the calculation shall be placed in a woodland conservation easement in order to preserve the trees for which they are getting credit. The developer shall submit a tree survey to indicate the forested area to be preserved and the drip line of trees. The line of the conservation easement shall be at least five (5) feet from any drive, foundation, walk, patio, pool, deck, or tennis court or other paved areas. It shall be at least ten (10) feet from any septic tank, tile field, or underground utility. Utility easements shall be excluded. The area under the drip line of trees in the conservation easement shall be measured and multiplied by sixteen (16) to determine the landscape volume. No canopy extending outside the conservation easement shall be counted, nor shall any tree with more than twenty (20) percent of its canopy outside the conservation area be given credit.

5-15-3: CALCULATING LANDSCAPE VOLUME ON OPEN SITES

The number of plant units for street trees and yard landscaping shall be used to calculate the landscape volume. Existing trees are addressed by 5-15-2. The total number of plant units proposed to be provided shall be calculated separately for street trees and yard landscaping. The street tree landscaping is required by the Village as a number of plants per 100 feet of street frontage, so the frontage of the lot shall be entered to determine the number of street tree plant units. The number of plant units per acre of pervious area shall be entered. It is assumed that a normal lot landscaping would result in about two (2) plant units per acre. When more plant units are proposed than this to raise the SVR, the additional planting warrants protection. When more than two (2) plant units per acre of yard are proposed, a conservation easement shall be required to ensure the trees are maintained over time. The street trees are required to be planted by the Village and are to be maintained by the landowners, so no special restrictions are needed to protect them. A minimum of sixteen hundred(1,600) square feet shall be reserved for each plant unit. More is required where the material is spread out. Where more than eight (8) plant units per acre are desired, planning commission approval shall be required to ensure the yard is not so densely shaded that the landowner will seek approval to remove trees.

5-15-4: COORDINATION WITH MONOTONY CODE

The monotony code requires that units be varied considerably with regard to roof height and encourages complex detailing and shapes. These elements tend to require large building volumes. It is not considered desirable to limit creativity in the development of alternative facades. Thus, if a developer has several facades for a given floor plan, they will be able to average the different alternative facades for a floor plan. The developer must submit a plan on how the average will be maintained.

The Too-Big House in a Rural Setting:
The Experience of Teton County, Wyoming

This rather simple ordinance is interesting because of the problems faced by this rural county after it became a home for the rich and famous. In the 1980s, the too-big house arrived in Teton County. This was clearly complicated by the damage that such units did to the scenic nature of this very beautiful county, with homes on ridgelines or in line with views of valleys or the Teton Range.

TETON COUNTY, WYOMING, DEVELOPMENT REGULATIONS, 1994

Section 2450. Maximum Scale of Development

A. *Residential Development.* Notwithstanding the development standards specified in Table 2400, Schedule of Dimensional Limitations, single-family development shall comply with the following standards:

1. **Habitable space.** The maximum amount of habitable space for a single-family dwelling, including associated accessory structures, is 8,000 square feet.

2. **Total square footage.** The total floor area of a single-family dwelling, including all associated accessory structures, shall not exceed 10,000 square feet.

This ordinance was challenged by a landowner who came in with a building permit for a house whose floor area was just under the 8,000 square foot maximum. The garage was designed to permit a second floor, although none was shown, and several other multi-story spaces existed. After receiving the certification of compliance from the county, a second floor was added over the garage and in several other spaces, resulting in a home that measured 11,000 square feet. A red tag was issued, and the landowner sued the county. The county countersued. A summary judgment was issued in favor of the landowner, and the county appealed to the Wyoming Supreme Court. The county eventually won.

The most important part of this case, however, was the finding regarding the contention by the developer that the regulations were illegal. The regulations grew out of extensive discussions of community character and rural character in the comprehensive plan, so there was a firm planning basis for the regulations. In addition, a study of the existing ranch homes that were the standard type of rural housing in the county showed that even with a building to house hired help, the maximum square footage allowed by the ordinance was reasonable.

Here is the way the Wyoming Supreme Court expressed its support for the validity of the county's 8,000-square-foot maximum house:

> Teton County chose to address the broad range of concerns and problems it faced with burgeoning development, in an area of unique natural beauty and the availability of only a very limited amount of privately-owned land, by adopting a comprehensive planning and zoning ordinance. All parties to the litigation agree that Teton County is unique in many ways and certainly one of only a handful of areas on earth with such an abundance of natural amenities. Teton County chose as one tool in its arsenal of weapons to prevent the destruction of those natural amenities a limitation on the square footage of new homes to 8,000 square feet. It might have opted for 5,000 square feet or it might have chosen 15,000 square feet, but it picked 8,000. A limitation of some sort is, without need of further justification, rational. In any event, we must give recognition to the fact that a limiting number of some sort is by its very nature reasonable in virtually any context, and, as will be shown from Teton County's planning process, painstaking thought went into selecting the "number." Clearly, the number cho-

sen provides for what can only be described as a house of commodious proportions, though it clearly does limit all persons' leave to a single family dwelling of such proportions that it can accommodate multiple generations of families or, for that matter, groups of unrelated individuals which might exceed the capacity of an 8,000 square foot house. Teton County intended that its regulations have such an effect, and we are convinced that a legitimate and rational purpose motivated the regulations. Among these rational and legitimate purposes are: (1) preserving community character; (2) preserving rural and western character; (3) promoting land use compatibility; (4) promoting housing affordability; and (5) mitigating against an unworkable increase in the number of low wage employees needed to provide services to, and maintain, large homes thereby lessening the demand for affordable housing in an area where affordable housing was scarce and getting scarcer." (*The Board of County Commissioners of Teton County, Wyoming v. Thomas L. Crow*, 65P.3d, 720)

The support for community character, specifically western and rural character, and affordable housing, as expressed in this ruling, shows the importance of a record of deliberation and a foundation in a comprehensive plan for the types of controls discussed in this PAS report.

It cannot be overemphasized that the most effective way to control teardowns is to anticipate the problem well in advance of the market, prior to the point where the first homes are torn down and replaced with too-big houses.

Another interesting aspect of the litigation is the landowner's argument about not affecting volume. The court in this case supports the choice of floor area. Nevertheless, this points up the problem of simple regulations. The consultants originally suggested a volume-based regulation that the county felt was too complex for people to understand. It is clear that a volume-based regulation would have prevented such a large building if based on an 8,000-square-foot building. It is also clear that the landowner designed the house to permit the additional floor area and intended to build a larger building from the start. In drafting regulations, it is always better to use more precise measures. It also eliminates inconsistencies. A home on a slope under the Teton County regulations achieves more floor area and volume because basement area does not count.

More detailed rules on measurement similar to those from Lake Forest that appear in the teardowns section below would have also prevented the problem. Both a volume approach and more complex measurements of floor area alternatives would have directly addressed the landowners' contention that floor area was immaterial because he did not alter the volume of the building.

REGULATIONS TO PRESERVE COMMUNITY CHARACTER IN THE FACE OF TEARDOWNS

It cannot be overemphasized that the most effective way to control teardowns is to anticipate the problem well in advance of the market, prior to the point where the first homes are torn down and replaced with too-big houses. A first step in the process of determining if a neighborhood is ripe for teardowns is to calculate the floor area permitted within the setbacks and to compare it with existing and proposed new homes in various residential districts. Every planning agency would be well served to go through this exercise. It clearly identifies the potential for teardowns and for other problems, such as where decks go when the building pad is full.

The first step is to do a maximum floor area calculation based on setbacks and compare that to the average buildings in the block. If old building permits or plans can be found, this will be much easier.

The second step is to compare maximum height regulations with what exists in the neighborhood. A major difference between possible and existing heights represents a potential character problem for the neighborhood if teardowns occur. If there is not a great gap, there is little to fear from teardowns unless there are unique architectural or history characteristics involved.

The third step is to look at what can be built in the setbacks: Is there room for decks or other elements commonly found in the neighborhood. If buildout eliminates typical outdoor facilities, some change in control is needed regardless of teardown potential. There are new neighborhoods where developers pack the site where variance requests poor in within a year.

Because teardowns typically occur on smaller lots that were developed 30 or more years ago, simple conventional regulations (see the subsections below) will be a better solution than more complex volume controls because they require only adjustments rather than a whole new generation of regulation. If regulations are changed only slightly, well before the first teardown, existing residents and home builders should not have any serious issues with the regulations. Completely new regulations generate more suspicion than modification of familiar regulations. Further, the effort of carefully explaining new concepts to existing residents is more is more challenging because new regulations always invoke fear. The exception is when new regulations are done as part of a comprehensive update of the code, which good planning practice dictates should occur every 10 years or so (in practice, regrettably, this occurs far less frequently). Where the standards are applied to the entire community, rather than just the neighborhoods in danger of teardowns, it reduces the reaction to change in a single neighborhood that the residents of that neighborhood feel when they think they've been singled out.

Setbacks and Height

The most likely condition is that the current regulations consist solely of setback and height regulations. They will need to be revised to conform to the houses that exist in the neighborhood (which are not necessarily built to those standards) in order to keep new houses that are replacing teardowns in character with neighborhood units.

The first stage in revising these regulations is to accurately determine the building coverage of current homes and to compare that against the setbacks as provided for in the zoning ordinance. This is best done with high-quality aerial photos or high-quality GIS data placing the building footprint directly on the lot. Height can be eyeballed by somebody familiar with building practice; a planner and building inspector can make close determinations with minimum actual measurements. If the jurisdiction has floor plans of typical units in the neighborhood in its files, these are far better.

The second step is to work out regulations to permit reasonable increases in house size so that genuine improvements in the community are possible. These expansions, however, must not destroy the community character. There is no model for determining what is a suitable expansion; some ranges need to be identified and imaging tools (e.g., build-out scenarios juxtaposing photos of existing units with proposed units) may be needed so that residents can measure the overall effect of change.

Adjusting setbacks may create problems for garages or patios. Fortunately, this can be easily alleviated. Most ordinances have a section spelling out permitted intrusions into setbacks for chimneys, roofs, stairs, and other elements. In increasing setbacks to limit house size, the impact on outdoor spaces or secondary buildings must be considered.

Adjusting height standards may be more difficult because it is likely that existing homes are substantially below the maximum allowable height predicated by the ordinance. A very common maximum height around the nation is 35 feet. Ranch houses built in the 1950s rarely even approach 20 feet. Cape Cods and split-levels or tri-levels are all going to have heights substantially lower than 35 feet. Reducing the height in neighborhoods of these housing types limits the detrimental effect teardowns could have on the neighborhood. Even in two-story neighborhoods, existing roof heights may be well below 35 feet due to shallower roof pitches than those currently popular.

Building Coverage and Floor Area Ratios

Again, there is no model language here because, if there are standards for building coverage and FAR, it is only a matter of adjusting the general ordinance standard to limit the size of houses sited on teardown sites. If a community is going to use one of these two standards in addition to the setback and height standards, there will need to be a careful study of the existing houses to determine what changes, including increases to the standards, should be allowed.

Overlay Districts

Because the neighborhood threatened with teardowns already exists, one very good way to implement standards to keep replacement houses in character with their neighbors is through an overlay district. If the current zoning is R-3, for example, this approach would create an R-3 overlay district to protect the character of the neighborhood. For example, an R-3 neighborhood of bungalows built from 1900 through 1930 will be very different in character from the R-3 subdivision built last year and needs standards in an overlay district that conform to that historical precedent.

The overlay permits the protection of a wide variety of neighborhoods. Once the standards for neighborhood types are identified, the critical element is the purpose statement for the overlay district. The purpose of the overlay is to protect the character of the existing neighborhood, which is built to a standard substantially lower than the one permitted by the district standards. In effect, the neighborhood is overzoned because out-of-scale buildings are actually permitted. Planners need to explain to citizens that the neighborhood has a different character than areas built to the district standards and that the reduced bulk standards are needed to preserve the character. It may be worth pointing out that there is no other district that would preserve lot size and limit the homes to a compatible size. It is not recommended to create a new zoning category, as this simply clutters the ordinance. The use(s) in the district will not change. Thus, the bulk standards for the overlay only add a line to a bulk and lot standards table.

Downzoning

In many older cities and some older suburbs, downzoning may be needed. In both Milwaukee and Chicago, which have both undergone comprehensive rezoning, whole blocks or portions of neighborhoods were often zoned far more intensively than the existing buildings. While downzoning is often opposed in suburban communities by landowners, in cities, protecting the character of an existing neighborhood of similar buildings is likely to garner far more support.

Neighborhood Conservation

Neighborhood conservation districts provide another option for dealing with the teardown phenomenon. This variant on the overlay district approach has been applied in two ways.

First, neighborhood conservation districts apply additional setback, floor area, or height standards for the neighborhoods built well below the maximum intensity of the zoning district. These are areas where the character would be damaged or destroyed by homes built to the maximum standards of the district. Such district designation is also useful where the zoning has changed over the years so that lots built under the old zoning became nonconforming under the new regulations.

Waiting Period

This approach attacks the economics of teardowns. Consider Lake Forest, Illinois, an old and noted Chicago rail suburb. While most new housing and much old housing is very large, a portion of the town dating back to its earliest period contains many small lots with modest homes. These houses were prime candidates for teardowns. Many, but not all, are protected by a historic district designation. The market is now bringing good housing of reasonable size into the teardown market.

Currently, the Lake Forest's code requires a two-year waiting period if a demolition permit is refused. The prospect of a two-year delay before tearing down a recently purchased building, and then subsequent delay in getting approval gives the city great negotiating strength to get architects to comply with city concerns about the building. The city has had regulations addressing the too-big house for many years.

LAKE FOREST, ILLINOIS, BUILDING CODE, 2003

This code excerpt contains architectural design, building scale, and demolition sections. It is a good example of the building scale approach that, while like Teton County relies on floor area, is crafted to better replicate volume than a simple floor area approach.

Section 9–86

B.   **ARCHITECTURAL DESIGN**. The City Council hereby finds that buildings, landscaping, awnings, signs, fences, and other structures, when designed within the context of the established surrounding neighborhood, preserve the character of the community, protect the unique aspects that distinguish neighborhoods from each other, provide for a diversity of house sizes at various price points, and maintain and enhance property values.

The surrounding neighborhood is defined as:
o The full block on which the property is located including both sides of the street.
o On a corner lot, the block face in both directions shall be considered.
o The adjoining block face to the rear of the property.
o The general character of the larger neighborhood, two blocks in each direction.

In reviewing a project, the following standards shall be considered. The Building Review Board shall from time-to-time develop design guidelines to further explain how these standards may appropriately be incorporated into a project, which guidelines shall be available from the Community Development Department. These standards and the illustrative design guidelines are provided to encourage strong design and to provide direction on how to achieve that goal. The standards are not intended to limit creativity or restrict the options for architectural styles.

Standard 1 - A style of architecture should be selected and all elevations and all elements of the building should be designed consistent with the chosen style.
Standard 2 - Siting of the development should be compatible with existing topography, existing trees and vegetation and the surrounding homes.
Standard 3 - Exterior elements of the structure including, but not limited to, roofs, entrances, eaves, chimneys, porches, and windows, should be of a human scale and designed within the context of the surrounding neighborhood.
Standard 4 - Materials and level of detailing and ornamentation should be consistent with the chosen style of architecture and the surrounding area.

Standard 5 -   Landscaping, fences and driveways should be designed in the context of the surrounding neighborhood and in a manner that is consistent with Chapter 42, Tree Preservation and Landscaping.

B.   **PURPOSE.** The City of Lake Forest is one of the oldest planned communities in the State of Illinois and it has grown in essential accord with its Comprehensive Plan. In order to preserve and protect the existing developed properties in the City, to maintain the Comprehensive Plan of the City to regulate development and to preserve and protect the public health, safety, and well-being, it is necessary to regulate building scale and environment.

The City of Lake Forest is experiencing unprecedented real estate development pressures. As a result, there is real concern with the scale of some of the new residences, additions to existing residences, and accessory structures within the City. In addition, there is concern about the impacts of infill development on the character and infrastructure in established neighborhoods.

It has been determined that the construction of large residences and accessory buildings that may be appropriate in estate settings are now being constructed on subdivision lots of inadequate area. The residences are often out of scale with the surrounding environment.

It is in the public interest of The City of Lake Forest to maintain an appropriate balance between building scale and the local environmental setting.

The City of Lake Forest is dedicated to maintaining the existing character and ambiance of the community. In the past, the City has encouraged a development pattern characterized as suburban estate wherein the landscape is generally dominant over the improvements. Now there is a significant trend to increase the size of residences in relation to the size of the lot. In addition, many sites under development are located in open spaces. The balance between landscaping and building scale in relation to space available is causing a noticeable change in the character of the community.

It is the intent of The City of Lake Forest to develop reasonable performance standards wherein the essential residential character of the City is maintained and fostered.

C.   **DEVELOPMENT REQUIREMENTS.**

1. Maximum Building Size.

The maximum building size is calculated based on the methodology established in Section 9-87D of this chapter. The Building Scale regulations apply to all single family homes and duplexes.

The maximum allowable square footage may be disapproved if the Board finds that the proposed residence or addition(s) are not in compliance with the design standards in Section 9-86 of the Building Code.

   a.   **Maximum Square Footage Allowances**
   i. <u>For lots of 18,900 square feet in area or smaller</u> –

   The maximum square footage of all structures on a zoning lot is determined by the following formula:

   Single Family and Duplex Dwelling
   (Lot area x .14) + 1,300 square feet

   ii. <u>For lots of 18,901 square feet to 40,000 square feet</u> –

   The maximum square footage of all structures on a zoning lot is determined by the following formula:

   Single Family Dwelling
   (Lot area x .05) + 3,000 square feet

   Duplex Dwelling
   (Lot area x .125) + 2,500 square feet

iii. <u>For lots larger than 40,000 square feet</u> –

The maximum square footage of all structures on a zoning lot is determined by the following formula:

Single Family Dwelling
(Lot area x .08) + 1,800 square feet
 Duplex   Dwelling
(Lot area x .125) + 2,500 square feet

b.   Basement Area Calculation
    i. Basements or portions of basements that extend above the adjacent ground area to a height of three and a half (3.5) feet or greater as measured from the top of the finished first floor to the lowest finished grade of the ground adjacent to the building, are included in the building scale calculation; provided, however, that such basement in dwellings constructed prior to January 9, 1989 shall be excluded from the building scale calculation.

EXHIBIT A

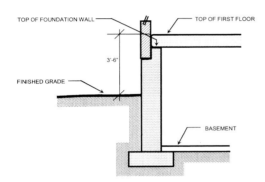

ii. Basements located wholly below grade and traditional window wells with a maximum width of 3 feet (3) are not included in the building scale calculation.

EXHIBIT B

COUNTED   NOT COUNTED   NOT COUNTED

iii. The portion of the basement included in the calculation shall be based on the extent of the basement above grade and shall be calculated as follows:

[TOTAL SQUARE FOOTAGE OF BASEMENT]
x
{[PERIMETER OF EXPOSED BASEMENT]
/PERIMETER OF ENTIRE BASEMENT]}

c.   **Second Floor and Attic Area Calculations**
The amount of second floor and third floor attic square footage
included in the building scale calculation is determined by the
second floor plate height and overall height of the residence. Attic
space may be factored into the calculations whether or not truss
construction is used.

i. <u>Second Floor Calculation</u>
Second floor area is included in the building scale calculation for
any section of the second floor lying beneath the plane formed by
the Second Floor Calculation Line and its intersection with any
exterior portions of the building (see illustration). The Second
Floor Calculation Line is measured from the top of first floor in
accordance with the following:

For all lot sizes, the Second Floor Calculation Line is 19 feet above
the top of first floor.

EXHIBIT C

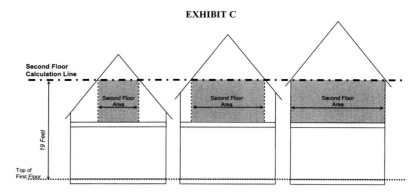

ii. <u>Third Floor Attic Calculation</u>
Third floor attic area is included in the building scale calculation
for any section of the attic lying beneath the plane formed by the
Attic Calculation Line and its intersection with any exterior
portions of the building (see illustration). The Attic Calculation
Line is measured from the top of first floor in accordance with the
following:

1.1   For Lots 40,000 square feet or smaller, the Attic
Calculation Line is 26.5 feet above the top of first floor.

1.2   For Lots 40,001 square feet or larger, the Attic Calculation
Line is 28 feet above the top of first floor.

EXHIBIT D

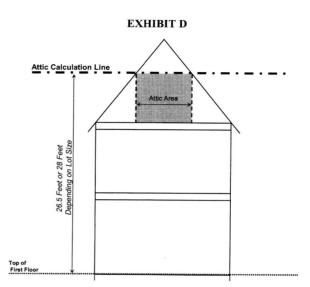

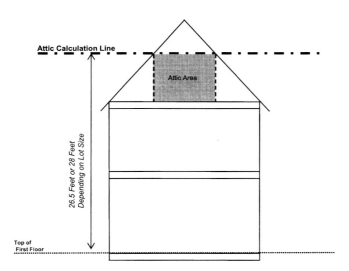

d. **Elements Exempted from the Above Calculations**
    i. <u>Garages</u>. In addition to the square footage permitted by the formulas in Section 9-87C1a above, each zoning lot shall be entitled to square footage for a garage in accordance with the following formulas.

    1.1   <u>For lots of 18,900 square feet in area or smaller</u> -- Garage Allowance: 576 square feet with a maximum width of 24 feet.
    1.2   <u>For lots of 18,901 to 40,000 square feet</u> -- Garage Allowance: 600 square feet
    1.3   <u>For lots larger than 40,000 square feet</u> -- Garage Allowance: 800 square feet
    1.4   Garages that exceed the allowable square footages may be constructed, but the square footage in excess of that allowed under Section 9-87C1d(i)(1.1 - 1.3) shall be deducted from the maximum square footage permitted for the residence. Prior to approval of a garage in excess of the allowable size, the project must be found to be in conformance with Section 9-86 of the City Code.

    ii. <u>Other Exemptions</u>. The following elements shall be exempted from the Building Scale calculation if the project is in conformance with Section 9-86 of the City Code and if the total square footage of these elements does not exceed 10% above the maximum allowable square footage for the residence.
        -- Front or Side Porch
        -- Covered Entry
        -- Portico
        -- Rear or Side Screen Porch
        -- Breezeways
        -- Pergola
        -- Individual Dormers
        -- Bay Windows

    The Director of Community Development shall be authorized to develop regulations to define further the foregoing elements, which regulations shall be set forth in a "Building Scale Methodology Document" that shall be available to the public from the Community Development Department.

iii. <u>Storage Sheds</u>. Storage sheds up to a maximum size of 100 square feet may be permitted if all other applicable provisions of the City Code are satisfied. Storage sheds shall not count toward the 10% overage allowed for the elements listed in Section 9-87C1d(ii) above.

2. Lot Area Calculation.

a. **Lot Area**

Lot area shall be determined by calculating the total square footage within the boundaries of the property lines based on as up-to-date official plat of survey. The plat survey must be prepared or updated by an Illinois registered land surveyor and contain, at a minimum, the following information:

i. Any lot which is not rectangular or which has easements for ingress and egress, natural and man made storm water retention ponds, or wetlands, shall have the lot area certified by the surveyor, including a detailed breakdown of square footage of lot area with, and without such easements, ponds, or wetlands.

ii. Full exterior dimensions of all existing structures on the property.

b. **Building Scale Calculation**

For the purposes of calculating building scale, the following areas are not included in determining total lot square footage.

i. The access easement for lots-in-depth shall not be included in the square footage for either the front or rear lot.

EXHIBIT E

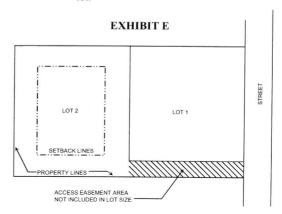

ii. 50% of any non-table land on the property as defined in Section 46-15 of the City Code. Certification of the total square footage by a Registered Land Surveyor may be required by the Director of Community Development.

EXHIBIT F

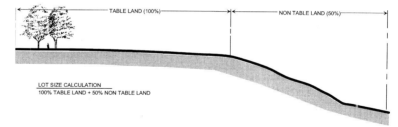

3. **Building Height.**
The maximum height of a single-family dwelling or two-family dwelling shall not exceed the following:

Lot Size	Maximum Height, Measured to the Ridge Line
18,900 square feet or less	30 feet
18,901 to 40,000 sq. ft.	35 feet
40,001 sq. ft. or greater	40 feet

For new construction, the top of first floor shall not be more than 1'-6" above the average finished grade adjacent to the building unless required under the provisions of the Lake County Watershed Development Ordinance.

Maximum height will be measured from the lowest grade immediately adjacent to the proposed structure, prior to construction, to the highest roof ridge line.

EXHIBIT G

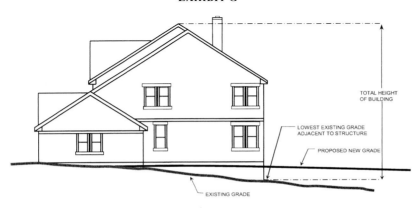

4. **Planned Residential Development Provisions.** In any subdivision involving a nonstandard single family development, including, but not limited to, a Planned Development, as permitted under Section 46-24 of the Zoning Code, or a Residential Open Space Subdivision, as permitted under Section 46-46 of the Zoning Code, the City shall, during the subdivision review process, establish a maximum floor area per lot for such development, consistent with the intent of this section and reflective of the uniqueness of the particular subdivision.

D. **EXCEPTIONS GRANTED BY BUILDING REVIEW BOARD.** The Building Review Board shall have the authority to grant exceptions to the maximum floor area requirements set forth in Section 9-87C, for a new residence or an addition to an existing residence if Standard 1 below is satisfied and at least one of the other Standards set forth in this Section 9-87D is met.

Standard 1 -- The project is consistent with the design standards in Section 9-86 of the City of Lake Forest Code.

Standard 2 -- Mature trees and other vegetation on the property effectively mitigate the appearance of excessive height and mass of the structure and as a result, the proposed development is in keeping with the streetscape and overall neighborhood.

Standard 3 -- New structures or additions are sited in a manner that minimizes the appearance of mass from the streetscape. In addition, the proposed structures or additions will not have a significant negative impact on the light to and views from neighboring homes.

Standard 4 -- The height and mass of the residence, garage, and accessory structures will generally be compatible with the height and mass of structures on adjacent lots, buildings on the street and on adjacent streets, and other residences and garages in the same subdivision.

Standard 5 – The property is located in a local historic district or is designated as a Local Landmark and the addition is consistent with the standards in the Historic Preservation Ordinance and approval of a variance would further the purpose of the ordinance.

Standard 6 – The property is adjacent to land used and zoned as permanent open space, a Conservation Easement, or a detention pond and the structures are sited in a manner that allows the open area to mitigate the appearance of mass of the buildings from the streetscape and from neighboring properties.

E. **APPLICATION FOR DEMOLITION PERMIT.** To permit adequate time for consideration of alternatives to demolition of an existing building(s), and to ensure development consistent with the goals of the City, a demolition permit shall be issued only after two years following an application for demolition unless one of the following exceptions shall cause said permit to be issued earlier.

1. Fire or other casualty damage or structural deterioration shall have rendered the structure and/or remains, in the opinion of the Director of Community Development of The City of Lake Forest, an immediate health or safety hazard. (Nothing in this section shall be deemed to limit the power of such official to condemn, and order the demolition of, any structure which is hazardous or unsafe.)

2. It is determined upon proper application for an exception, and following a public hearing by the Building Review Board, in consideration of the criteria and purpose of this section and Section 46-27 (Historic Residential and Open Space Preservation) of the Zoning Code, that a delay in demolition would not further the purpose of this section and Section 46-27 of the Zoning Code, because;

    a. The structure itself, or in relation to its environs, has no significant historical, architectural, aesthetic or cultural value in its present or restored condition; or

    b. Realistic alternatives (including adaptive uses) are not likely because of the nature or cost of work necessary to preserve such structure or realize any appreciable part of such value; or

    c. The structure in its present or restored condition is unsuitable for residential, or a residentially compatible use; or

    d. The demolition is consistent with, or materially furthers, the criteria and purpose of this section and Section 46-27 of the Zoning Code.

3. It is determined by the City Manager that the issuance of a demolition permit is clearly consistent with the criteria of this section and Section 46-27 of the Zoning Code.

    In cases where the applicant for demolition permit intends to construct a replacement building(s), neither the Building Review Board nor the City Manager shall have authority under paragraphs E(2) or E(3), immediately above, to exempt any applicant from the two year waiting period imposed by this sub-section, unless the applicant shall have first obtained approval by the Building Review Board of any such replacement building(s), in accordance with the criteria set forth in Section 9-86 above. Additionally, any new building sought to be constructed as a replacement building after demolition, as permitted under this section, shall require advance approval by the Building Review Board in accordance with Section 9-86 above, prior to the issuance of a building permit.

CONCLUSION

A major challenge to new and old communities across the nation is to maintain the character of the community or neighborhood. For green field development, the threat is primarily in the form of monotony, monopoly set houses, and the too-big house. For the existing neighborhood, teardowns or changes in character from zoning changes are the primary threat. The zoning change issue is not addressed here as it is standard current planning practice to address that concern, and every ordinance has processes to review zoning changes.

The tools contained herein offer a variety of ways to address the problems and can be incorporated into existing zoning, land development, or subdivision regulations. They vary from simple camouflage with landscaping to detailed review strategies.

The major exception to the regulatory approach is with teardowns. Teardowns are, for the most part, linked to an overheated economic condition that renders the neighborhood obsolete. It is a problem that can be anticipated in communities with small houses. These neighborhoods have charm; otherwise, they would not be desirable in many cases. Planning can provide a means to upgrade without teardowns that totally alter the character, but it must occur before the economics create a demand for teardowns.

The other element that cannot easily be regulated is the too-big house. Bigger is not always better, but planners, architects, and the press need to change opinions so that smaller, more attractive homes with great style are built, rather than starter castles and McMansions.

Bibliography

Duchscherer, Paul, and Douglas Keister. 1995. *The Bungalow: America's Arts & Crafts Home.* New York: Penguin Books.

Friedman, Avi. 2002. *Planning the New Suburbia. Flexibility by Design.* Vancouver: University of British Columbia Press.

Kendig, Lane. 1980. *Performance Zoning.* Chicago: Planners Press.

Ross, Lynn M. 2003. "Zoning Affordability: The Challenges of Inclusionary Housing." *Zoning News,* August.

Susanka, Sarah. 2002. *Creating the Not So Big Housed: Insights and Ideas for the New America Home.* Newton, Conn.: Taunton Press.

Susanka, Sarah, with Kira Obolensky. 2001. *The Not So Big House: A Blueprint for the Way We Really Live.* Newton, Conn.: Taunton Press.

Tolpin, Jim. 1998. *The New Cottage Home.* Newton, Conn.: Taunton Press.

MAKING GREAT COMMUNITIES HAPPEN

The American Planning Association provides leadership in the development of vital communities by advocating excellence in community planning, promoting education and citizen empowerment, and providing the tools and support necessary to effect positive change.

474/475. Online Resources for Planners. Sanjay Jeer. November 1997. 126pp.

476. Nonpoint Source Pollution: A Handbook for Local Governments. Sanjay Jeer, Megan Lewis, Stuart Meck, Jon Witten, and Michelle Zimet. December 1997. 127pp.

477. Transportation Demand Management. Erik Ferguson. March 1998. 68pp.

478. Manufactured Housing: Regulation, Design Innovations, and Development Options. Welford Sanders. July 1998. 120pp.

479. The Principles of Smart Development. September 1998. 113pp.

480/481. Modernizing State Planning Statutes: The Growing Smart^{SM} Working Papers. Volume 2. September 1998. 269pp.

482. Planning and Zoning for Concentrated Animal Feeding Operations. Jim Schwab. December 1998. 44pp.

483/484. Planning for Post-Disaster Recovery and Reconstruction. Jim Schwab, et al. December 1998. 346pp.

485. Traffic Sheds, Rural Highway Capacity, and Growth Management. Lane Kendig with Stephen Tocknell. March 1999. 24pp.

486. Youth Participation in Community Planning. Ramona Mullahey, Yve Susskind, and Barry Checkoway. June 1999. 70pp.

489/490. Aesthetics, Community Character, and the Law. Christopher J. Duerksen and R. Matthew Goebel. December 1999. 154pp.

493. Transportation Impact Fees and Excise Taxes: A Survey of 16 Jurisdictions. Connie Cooper. July 2000. 62pp.

494. Incentive Zoning: Meeting Urban Design and Affordable Housing Objectives. Marya Morris. September 2000. 64pp.

495/496. Everything You Always Wanted To Know About Regulating Sex Businesses. Eric Damian Kelly and Connie Cooper. December 2000. 168pp.

497/498. Parks, Recreation, and Open Spaces: An Agenda for the 21st Century. Alexander Garvin. December 2000. 72pp.

499. Regulating Home-Based Businesses in the Twenty-First Century. Charles Wunder. December 2000. 37pp.

500/501. Lights, Camera, Community Video. Cabot Orton, Keith Spiegel, and Eddie Gale. April 2001. 76pp.

502. Parks and Economic Development. John L. Crompton. November 2001. 74pp.

503/504. Saving Face: How Corporate Franchise Design Can Respect Community Identity (revised edition). Ronald Lee Fleming. February 2002. 118pp.

505. Telecom Hotels: A Planners Guide. Jennifer Evans-Crowley. March 2002. 31pp.

506/507. Old Cities/Green Cities: Communities Transform Unmanaged Land. J. Blaine Bonham, Jr., Gerri Spilka, and Darl Rastorfer. March 2002. 123pp.

508. Performance Guarantees for Government Permit Granting Authorities. Wayne Feiden and Raymond Burby. July 2002. 80pp.

509. Street Vending: A Survey of Ideas and Lessons for Planners. Jennifer Ball. August 2002. 44pp.

510/511. Parking Standards. Edited by Michael Davidson and Fay Dolnick. November 2002. 181pp.

512. Smart Growth Audits. Jerry Weitz and Leora Susan Waldner. November 2002. 56pp.

513/514. Regional Approaches to Affordable Housing. Stuart Meck, Rebecca Retzlaff, and James Schwab. February 2003. 271pp.

515. Planning for Street Connectivity: Getting from Here to There. Susan Handy, Robert G. Paterson, and Kent Butler. May 2003. 95pp.

516. Jobs-Housing Balance. Jerry Weitz. November 2003. 41pp.

517. Community Indicators. Rhonda Phillips. December 2003. 46pp.

518/519. Ecological Riverfront Design. Betsy Otto, Kathleen McCormick, and Michael Leccese. March 2004. 177pp.

520. Urban Containment in the United States. Arthur C. Nelson and Casey J. Dawkins. March 2004. 130pp.

521/522. A Planners Dictionary. Edited by Michael Davidson and Fay Dolnick. April 2004. 460pp.

523/524. Crossroads, Hamlet, Village, Town (revised edition). Randall Arendt. April 2004. 142pp.

525. E-Government. Jennifer Evans–Cowley and Maria Manta Conroy. May 2004. 41pp.

526. Codifying New Urbanism. Congress for the New Urbanism. May 1997. 97pp.

527. Street Graphics and the Law. Daniel Mandelker with Andrew Bertucci and William Ewald. August 2004. 133pp.

528. Too Big, Boring, or Ugly: Planning and Design Tools to Combat Monotony, the Too-big House, and Teardowns. Lane Kendig. December 2004. 103pp.